Masaccio

Cecilia Frosinini

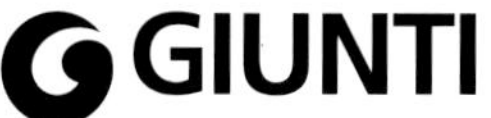

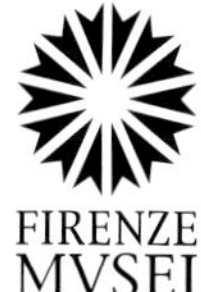

Graphic design: Giovanni Breschi

Translation: Michael Sullivan
for NTL, Florence

Cover: *The bestowing of alms
and the death of Ananias*,
detail, c. 1424-1426.
Florence, Brancacci Chapel.

Reprint	Year
6 5 4 3 2 1 0	2007 2006 2005 2004 2003

Contents

The artist's life

4 The early years

10 Brunelleschi and the Florentine milieu

18 The collaboration with Masolino

34 In Rome

42 *Chronology*

The Masterpieces

44 San Giovenale Triptych

48 Brancacci Chapel

56 Pisa Polyptych

62 *Index of names and bibliography*

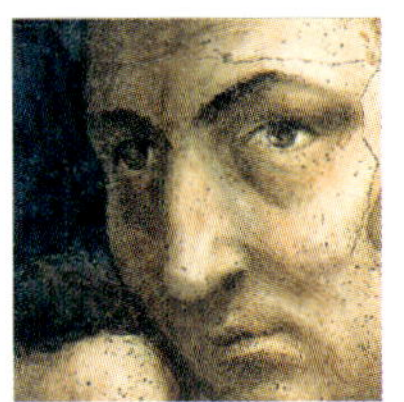# The early years

Tommaso di ser Giovanni da Castel San Giovanni, already known to his contemporaries as Masaccio ("not at all because he was vice-ridden, since he was goodness itself, but because of his great negligence", "because he never wanted to think at all in any way about the cares and things of the world, and hardly about dressing itself", according to the words of Vasari), was born in Castel San Giovanni, the present-day San Giovanni Valdarno, a castle of the republic of Florence at the time, to a bourgeois family undoubtedly of considerable income. His father, Ser Giovanni di Mone d'Andreuccio, practised the profession of notary, an indication of high economic standing, but also of notable cultural acquirements got through higher studies. His profession had been made possible by the solid economic position of the paternal family, whose trade was that of "cassai", modern furniture-makers.

Married to his almost contemporary Monna Jacopa, originally from Barberino di Mugello, Ser Giovanni had three children by her: Tommaso, born on the feastday of St Thomas the Apostle (21 December) in 1401; Alessandra; and Giovanni, who saw the light after the death of Ser Giovanni in 1406, and who was given his father's name in memory of him. Masaccio's life thus began with a sudden change of fortune which, however, apart from family feeling, must not have had too great an effect on the boy's life. Tommaso likely lived with his father's family, expecially after his mother remarried, around 1412, to a wealthy widower, Tedesco di Maestro Feo, who traded as a druggist. It was once thought that Masaccio went with his mother to his step-father's home, on the basis of a document of his brother, the Giovanni who became a painter in his turn and is known as "Lo Scheggia". In his tax declaration of 1469 he states that "my mother remarried and she brought me up". But we learn nothing from him about the childhood of his elder brother, Masaccio: who, more than ten years old at

In this detail of the scene of the acknowledgment of St Peter's authority by the early Christian Church, Masaccio has inserted some portraits of the artists contemporary to him, among whom can be recognised Leon Battista Alberti and Filippo Brunelleschi. The young man looking at the viewer is unequivocably a self-portrait of the painter.

the time of their mother's second marriage, may have stayed with his father's family, while the younger Giovanni joined their mother in the new family nucleus. The fact that orphaned children stayed with the father's family was very usual in a patriarchal society like that of the time, to the point of making it necessary clarify explicitly when an anomalous situation occurred, as in the case of Lo Scheggia. It was indeed unlikely that a second husband would want to burden himself with three orphans; as it was quite as usual for the dead man's family to try to use emotional blackmail on the widow to prevent her, by remarrying, from diminishing the family fortune, given that she had the right to the restitution of her dowry. To all these considerations should be added others that make it plausible that

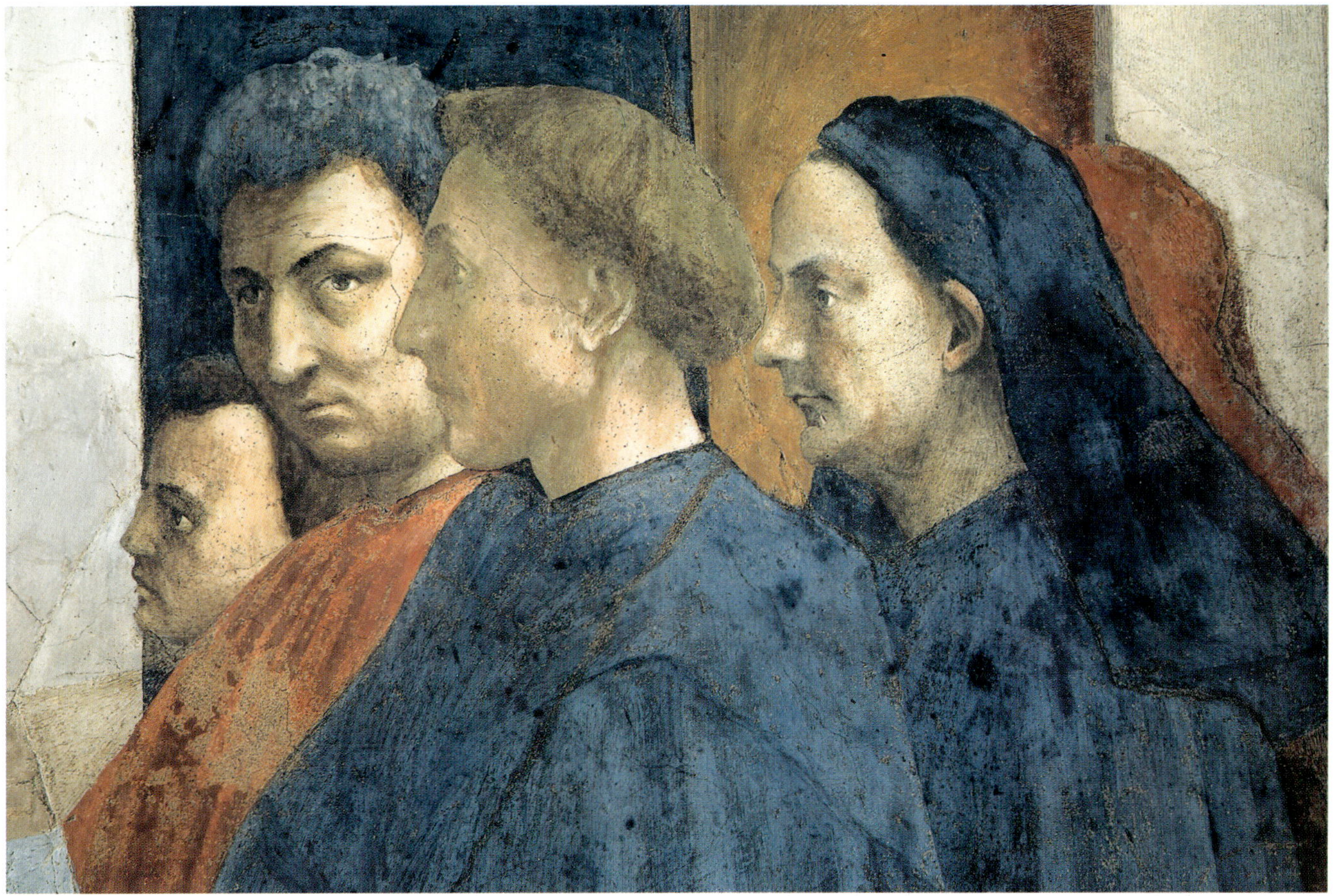

Masaccio did stay with his father's family as a boy: and that is the fact that he certainly received considerable schooling, similar to that which his father had received in his time, as emerges from a careful scrutiny of the documents he produced in his own hand.

One of the nodal points in the brief life story of Masaccio remains that of his artistic training. There have been numerous hypotheses suggested by critics, beginning with the "shortcut", coming from Vasari, who interpreted the privileged relation of collaboration between Masolino and Masaccio as that of master and apprentice, down to the more modern studies aimed at picking out a name from the artistic panorama of Florence in the second decade of the fifteenth century. Since obviously there was no possibility of finding a painter of the generation prior to him who could have been his master in the full sense of the term, given the enormous gap between Masaccio's first public offering, the *San Giovenale Triptych*, dated 1422, and Florentine painting of the same period, suggestions have concentrated on the names of absolutely second-rate figures from the artistic point of view, who however had some remote documentary tie with Masaccio and of whom people limited themselves to thinking that they might, if nothing else, have offered a base to the young man just arrived from his native Castel San Giovanni; figures such as those of Mariotto di Cristofano (1393-1457) and of Bicci di Lorenzo (1373-1452).

The first of the two, Mariotto, had married a young woman of Castel San Giovanni, Caterina, daughter of the first marriage of Tedesco di Feo. Careful examination of the documents on the history of Masaccio's family enables us however to see that the ties of "kinship" between the two artists came into being only at a time at which Masaccio must necessarily have already been an autonomous artist and hence no longer in need of a master, since Mariotto married Caterina only in 1421.

It was certainly not a period of engagements understood in the Romantic-nineteenth century sense, long courtships and hence family relationships before marriage which, on the contrary, were contracts of economic or associative convenience. Furthermore, relations between the family of the heirs of the druggist Tedesco and Monna Jacopa, Masaccio's mother, were always tense, in that they were complicated by everlasting quarrels over questions of inheritance. Masaccio, and then his brother Giovanni, found themselves acting as legal representatives for their mother in numerous disputes that ended up in court and even resulted in the imprisonment of some of the litigants.

The other name that has been advanced in suggesting a Florentine milieu for Masaccio as adolescent is that of Bicci di Lorenzo, a prolific artist who ran a traditional workshop, of the family kind, that had great success with all classes in the city and the rich countryside that served it, and that created, precisely because of its great good luck, a sort of highly recognisable artistic language, a Florentine late Gothic *koiné*.

As for Bicci, the historical reason for considering him a candidate lies in the fact that in 1421 and 1422 he had Masaccio's brother Lo Scheggia among the lads in his workshop. As things stand, precisely because of the silence of the documents, which are very detailed and rich as regards the workshop of Bicci di Lorenzo, one is inclined to exclude the possibility that

Facing page, clockwise:
Portrait of Masaccio, from *Lives of the most excellent painters, sculptors and architects* by Giorgio Vasari, 1568.

The tribute, detail, c. 1424-1426. Florence, Brancacci Chapel.

St Peter healing the sick with his shadow, detail, c. 1424-1426. Florence, Brancacci Chapel.

There is also a tradition that identifies in the figure of St Thomas, in the scene of the *Tribute*, a formal and idealised self-portrait of Masaccio that well fits the dominant position Vasari decided to give the painter in the biographies of the *Lives*. In the fair-haired and slim young man who follows St Peter in the scene of the *Healing with his shadow*, one sees the portrait of Giovanni di ser Giovanni, brother of Masaccio. The looks are extremely similar to those of the genuine self-portrait of Masaccio and well suit the nickname given him, Scheggia, which means a slender young fellow.

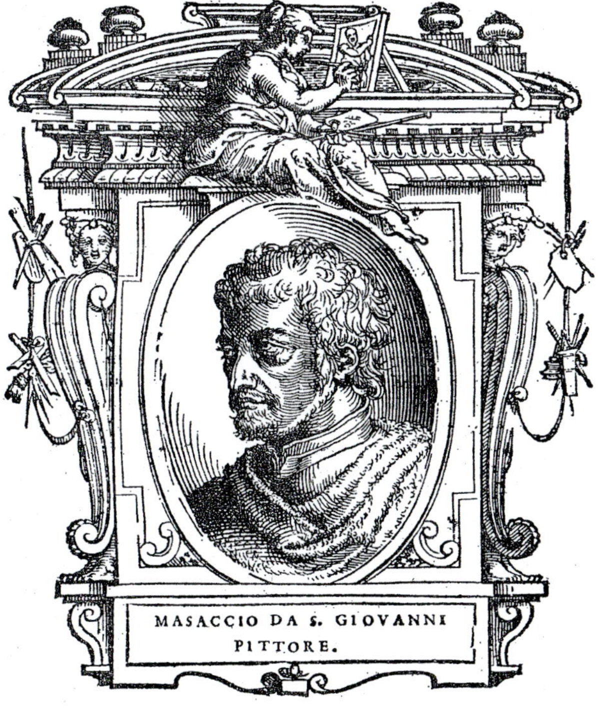

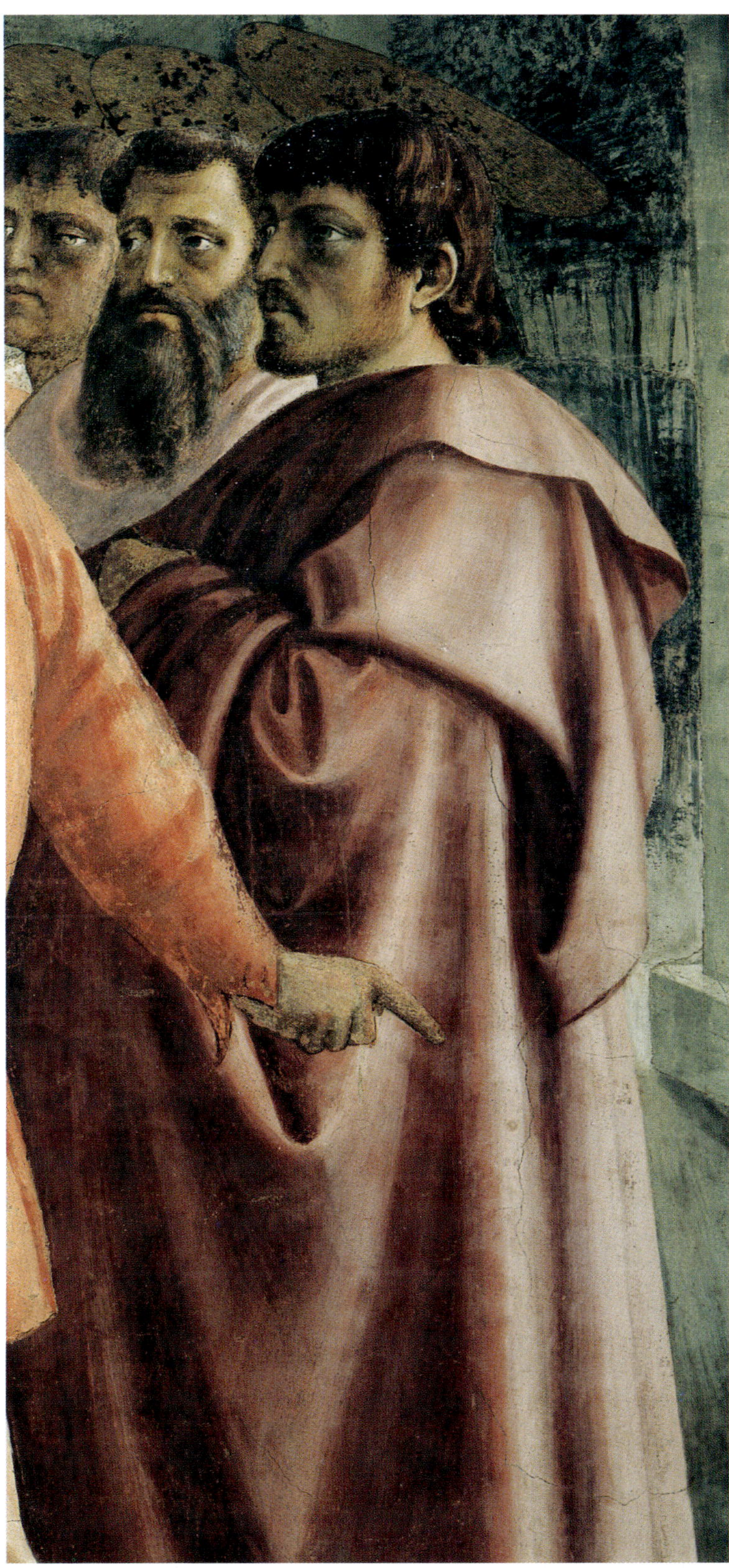

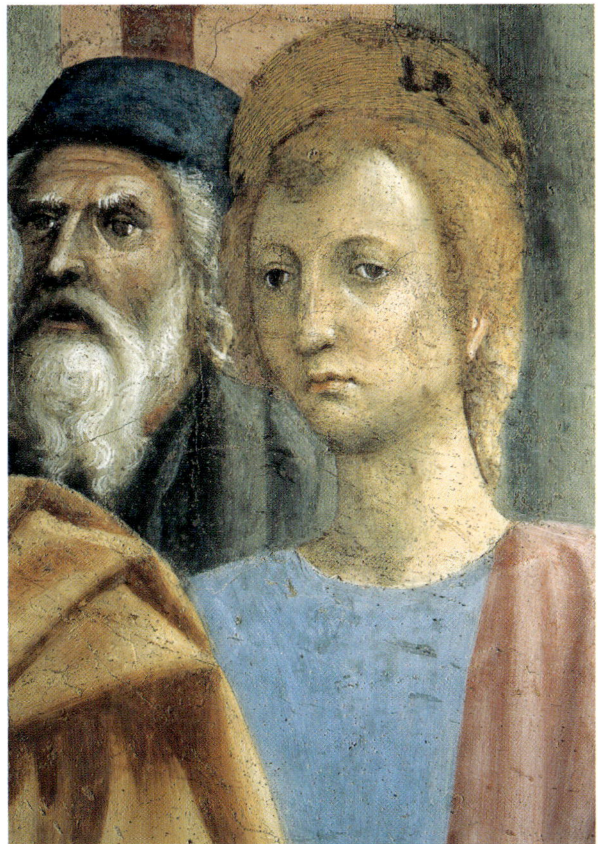

Masaccio could have passed through there without leaving some trace in the documentation. The fact that Masaccio settled his brother there for a short time could well have been an astute professional choice, since it was one of most suitable places in the Florence of the time to chose for a lad's apprenticeship. And Masaccio does not show, in his brief career, any interest in playing guide to the young. He did take on helpers who had already passed through the apprenticeship stage, like his own brother, some years later, in 1426, during his time in Pisa; and the not much older Andrea di Giusto Manzini (documented from 1424-1450).

To assess other hypotheses it is necessary to stress that research into Masaccio's art training did in Florence suffers from a double defect: on the one hand that of endorsing a very centralised and Florence-centred view of the situation of the craft; on the other that of introducing a chronological problem hard to solve. Masaccio's presence in Florence can, in fact, be traced with documentary certainty only to the period after 1417 (and in any case before 1421). Whereas we know from another source that already in 1418 Masaccio was described as "dipintore" and that he enjoyed good financial and social standing, given that he acted as guarantor for a master woodworker of Castel San Giovanni. This is perfectly compatible with the social situation of the time, that required apprenticeship to a trade to begin at a rather precocious age and that it be a fairly long phase of life. According to the *Libro dell'Arte* by Cennino Cennini, the contemporary treatise on painting technique, "as soon as you can, begin to put yourself under the guide of the master to learn; and leave the master as late as you can"; and the legislation of the Arte dei Medici e Speziali, the guild in which painters were enrolled, also established that apprenticeship should last at least seven years. Thus of necessity we must seek in Castel San Giovanni the location and occasion of Masaccio's technical training since on his arrival in Florence he was already at least seventeen and was shortly to begin to operate as an independent master.

That the youngster was set to the trade in his native town is altogether possible, given also the multiple work relations that his father's family could have had with the world of painters. The trade of chest-makers, exercised both by his grandfather and his uncle was, in fact, closely correlated to that of the painters. Not only did the chest-makers supply a raw material directly linked to painted decoration, but often the documents tell us the name of painters who describe themselves as "forzerinai" or "cassai" (strongbox- or chest-makers) citing the custom of many of these masters to enrol also or exclusively in the Arte dei Legnaiuoli, alongside carpenters producing furniture, an indication of a continual interaction between the two trades. As for that, to underline the high probability of the hypothesis that Masaccio was apprenticed to a strongbox-maker, it is to be remembered that Lo Scheggia, his brother, was enrolled as woodworker, as well as painter, and was mostly involved with painted chests.

Masaccio's mother's second husband, the well-off Tedesco di Feo, was engaged in a profession linked to the artistic world, that of druggist: a sort

Christus patiens between the Virgin and St Lucy by Mariotto di Cristofano, in the Museum of Santa Maria delle Grazie in San Giovanni Valdarno, 1420-1425.

Enthroned Madonna and Child and a donor by Bicci di Lorenzo, now in the Museum of the Collegiata in Empoli, 1423.

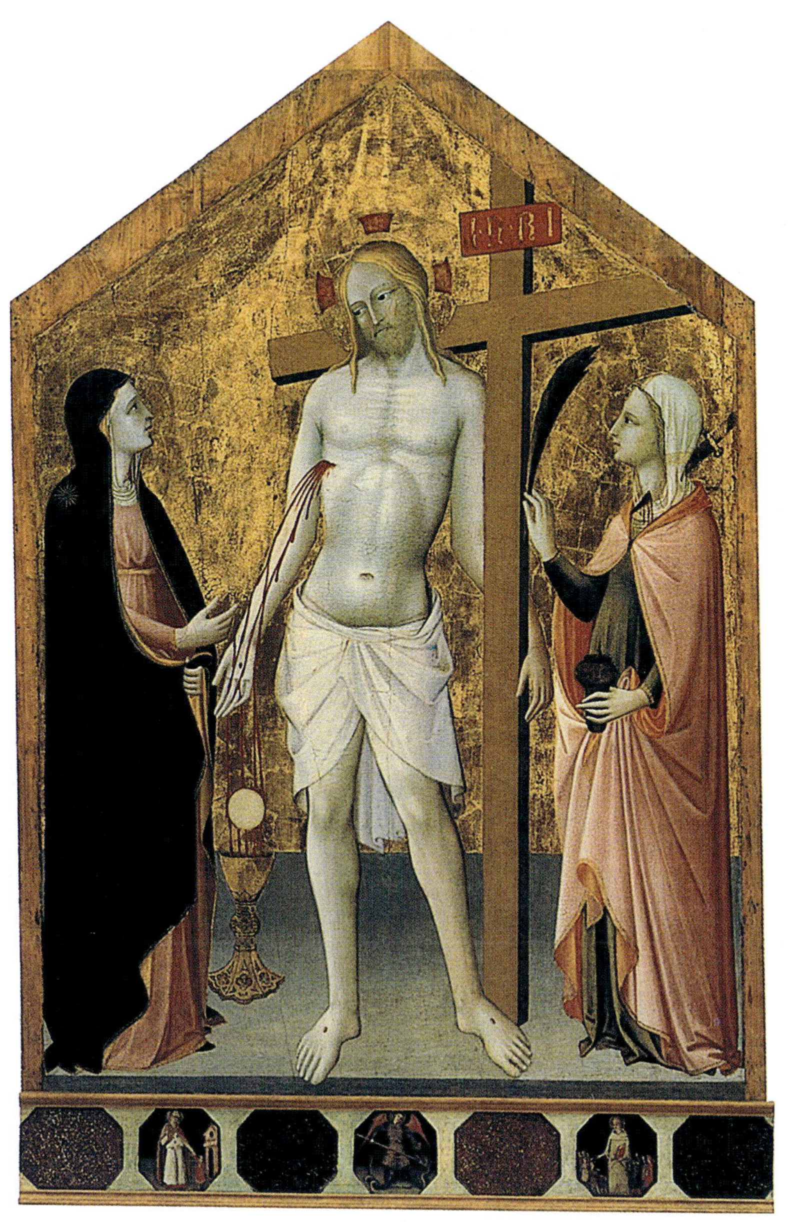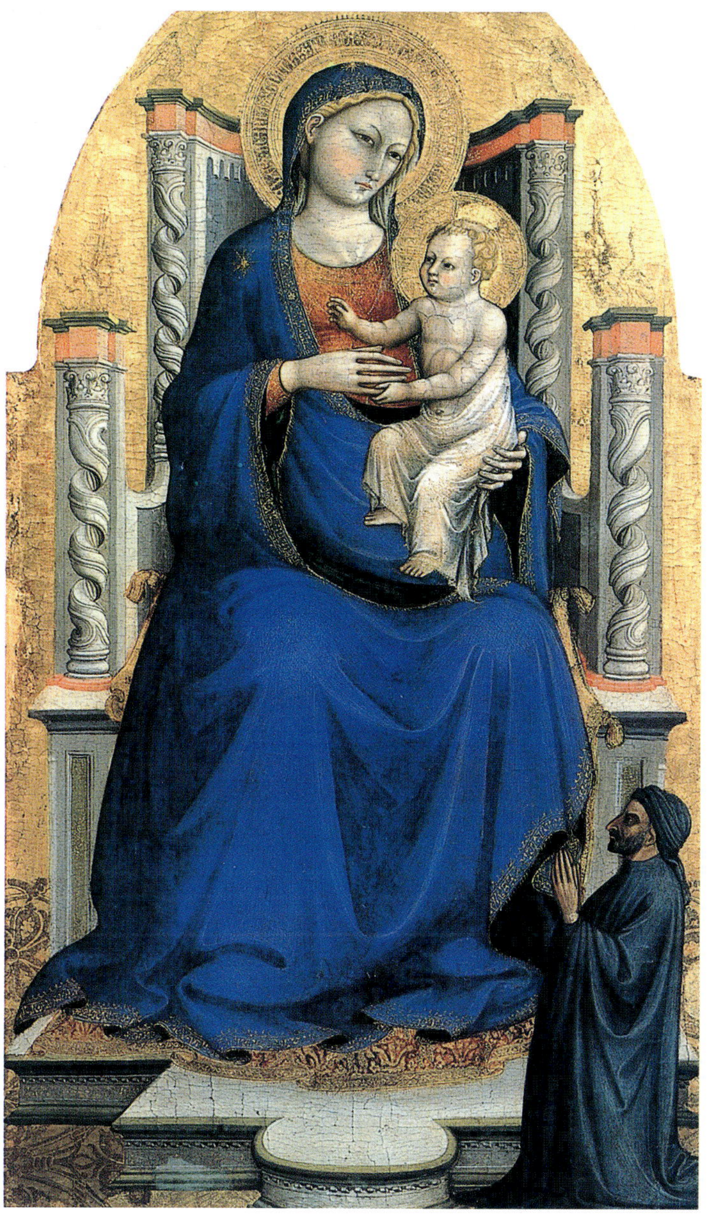

of pharmacist at the time, a druggist sold colours and other raw material to the artists. However since the marriage took place around 1412, one has to consider that at the time Masaccio must have already begun his apprenticeship, and so was likely under the aegis of his father's family with whom he was living. The work relations of his stepfather may at most have widened his circle of acquaintanceship but not have been their origin.

Another hypothesis should, however, be considered among the several already proposed in search of a place or an occasion for an apprenticeship to art for the young Masaccio, a hypothesis that takes into consideration the Florentine notarial milieu. The profession of the artist's father, in fact, though he died very young, would have put him in contact with workshops of paper-makers and illuminators. But I shall return to this point later.

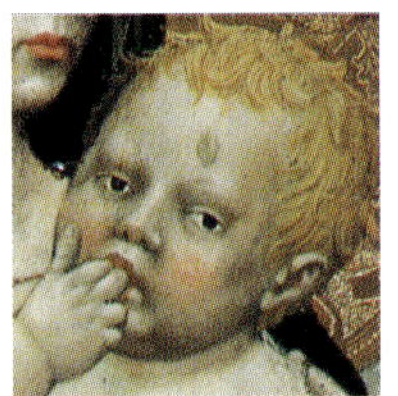

Brunelleschi
and the Florentine milieu

About the places Masaccio frequented in Florence we only know that his first dwelling was in the Parish of San Niccolò Oltrarno. From at least 1426 Masaccio then moved to the Parish of San Michele Visdomini, in Via de' Servi, while the sole workshop that the documents connect to his name is that in the area of Sant'Apollinare, shared from at least 1425 with another painter, Niccolò di ser Lapo. It was one of the buildings rented out by the monks of the Badia Fiorentina as workshop in the area below the monastery dormitory, close to the many trades of paper-makers, binders, illuminators, calligraphers directly linked to the numerous commissions of library material from the Benedictine monastery, but also to the Arte dei Notai. We do not know whether this was Masaccio's workplace in Florence from the beginning nor whether, as recently suggested, the Florentine master of Masaccio was indeed Niccolò di ser Lapo, much older than him.

At that time Florence was a rich and cosmopolitan city that attracted foreign painters and different experiences, even though under the strict control of the Arte dei Medici e Speziali which tended to watch over Florentine artists, keeping for all intents and purposes to the prohibitionist regime of late medieval artisan culture. The artistic milieu which Masaccio found on his arrival in Florence was strongly permeated by a late Gothic atmosphere, not only in the softened, Florentine version of Lorenzo Monaco, but also in an international one such as that of Starnina, back from a long stay in Spain; or enlivened by the Spanish asperities of Alvaro Pirez. But 1417, the year in which Masaccio came to Florence, was also the year in which Brunelleschi began to plan the dome of the cathedral. In 1418 the Arte di Calimala, the rich Florentine merchants' guild, pledged to finance the building. In 1419 work began on the Spedale degli Innocenti, again to Brunelleschi's design, and from 1420 on the dome. There were the years in which the still new statues of the Evangelists on the facade of the cathedral were looked at with won-

Madonna of Humility by Gherardo Starnina, in the Uffizi Gallery, Florence, c. 1403.

Coronation of the Virgin by Lorenzo Monaco, detail, in the Uffizi Gallery, Florence, 1414.

A masterpiece of Florentine late Gothic, the triptych brings together richness of working, profusion of precious materials and a range of technical skills with astute innovations, such as the unified field and the choice of a narrative scene instead of the more traditional throned Virgin with saints. Lorenzo Monaco shows himself to have been aware and responsive to the possibilities of a renewal in his art in a Florentine context of which he remains the finest exponent.

dering admiration, in which Donatello worked on the six statues of the Prophets for Giotto's Campanile, in which the niches of the Guilds outside the church of Orsanmichele were populated with enormous sculptures. These were the years of Donatello, of Lorenzo Ghiberti, of Nanni di Banco. On the basis of their profound rethinking of the antique, with them was born a quest for attitudes in statuary that expressed the new humanist conception and the virtue of dignity and self-awareness which that ideal endorsed. A statuary that went back to representing bodies made up of volumes, with the garments that covered them made of cloth and endowed with weight. A sculpture that early on gave artistic translation to Brunelleschi's perspective experiments, as shown by the *St George* altarpiece for one of the tabernacles

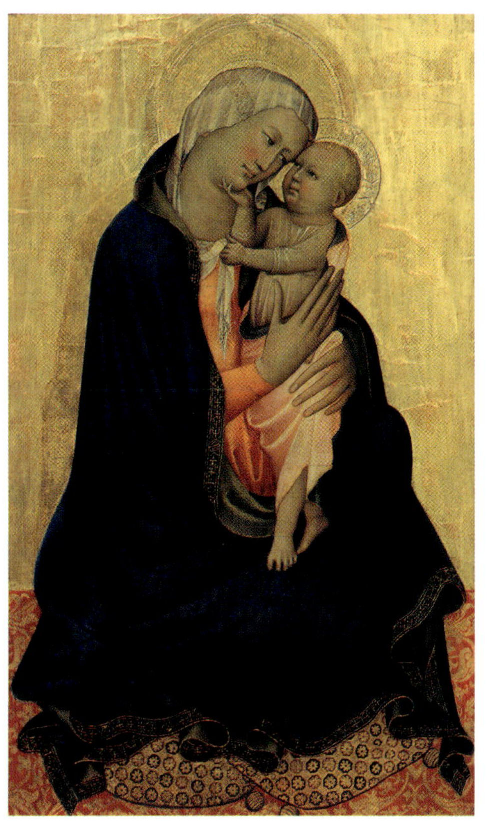
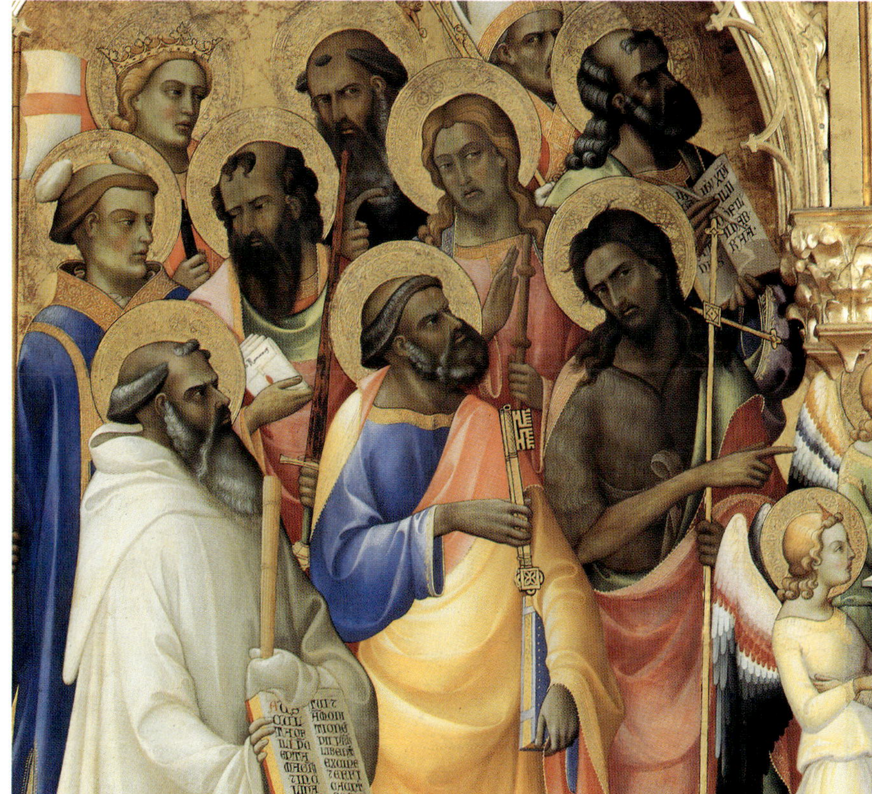

of Orsanmichele, on which Donatello worked in 1417. There was thus more than painting to be looked at, in those years, for a young man already trained, who had eyes to see and mind to understand. With good reason Vasari, unable to find a name among the painters of the time, attributes the development Masaccio's artistic conception to Brunelleschi and Donatello. An idea happily taken up by modern criticism, whereby Longhi categorically states that "if there was ever an artist who came out armed and ready from the brain of painting, it was Masaccio. That is why a prehistory for Masaccio in painting makes no sense". And Berenson before him had glimpsed the point, expressing it in the succint "Giotto reborn", meaning that only the study, the direct rethinking, of Giotto could have been master to Masaccio.

The concordance of written and material documents after his arrival in Florence forces us to believe in his prior engagement in the trade and a financial concreteness that permitted him to engage in legal proceedings atypical for a young artisan at the beginning of his career, in particular the previously mentioned payment to the Arte dei Legnaiuoli on behalf of an artisan of Castel San Giovanni: to make himself guarantor for someone else he had to be able to offer credit warranted by steady money-making activity or reliance on family wealth. Furthermore in January 1422 Masaccio enrolled in the Arte dei Medici e Speziali. There was no reason why a young artist should enrol except to get legal backing for an activity of a certain bulk. The majority of painters, in fact enrolled as late as possible and often preferred to depend for years on some older painter before striking out on their own. In the thinking of the time it was worth taking on the expense of the enrolment fee only when one couldn't do otherwise. We do not know what Masaccio had produced up to then but his first known work, the *Triptych* for the little church of San Giovenale, reveals, technically speaking, an already consummate artist, master of many skills of the trade (pp. 44-47). Certainly here Masaccio, barely twenty-one, had not only a sound financial position, but also solid experience behind him. The *Triptych* is dated 23 April 1422, three months after his enrolment, but it must have already been in progress (if not finished) in January of that year. Masaccio shows he had an early need for independence and artistic autonomy that made staying with an older master, as was the custom, unacceptable to him.

It was probably shortly after his arrival in Florence that Masaccio met Brunelleschi. The occasion of the meeting might have been their belonging, through their fathers' profession, to the notarial milieu. This was one of the most respected professions in the society of the time, one of those that required a longer *cursus studiorum* and serious cultural preparation. It seems also to have been the case, going from documents and analyses of social patterns, that admission to the restricted entourage continued to be reserved to members of the family of a notary even after the latter's death. It is no accident that both Masaccio and his brother continued to call themselves for life with their own name followed by the patronymic "di ser Giovanni". One could give innumerable other examples, but limiting oneself to Masaccio's circle of acquaintance it is enough to cite the already mentioned painter with whom he shared the Sant'Apollinare workshop, Niccolò, always recorded in contemporary documents as "di ser Lapo"; and Brunelleschi, who was all his life "Filippo di ser Brunellesco". No doubt it was the social aspirations of the family that provided Masaccio with the good educational level that emerges from the "portata" (tax declaration) he wrote to the land registry in 1427. Proba-

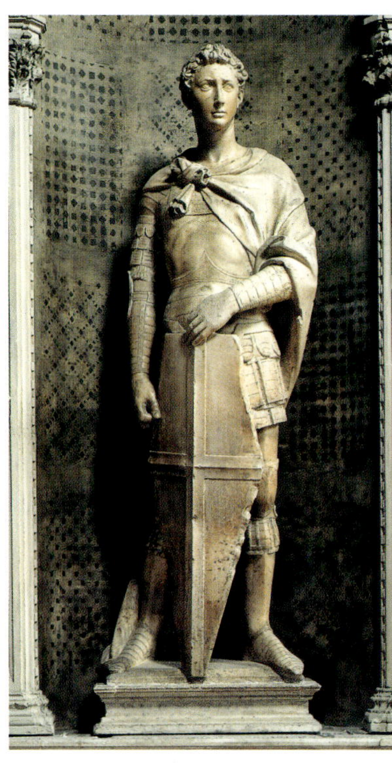

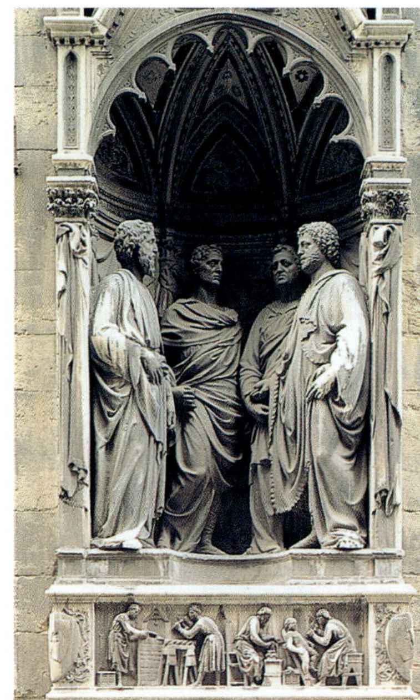

Above:
Four crowned Saints, by Nanni di Banco for a niche in the church of Orsanmichele in Florence, 1412-1416.

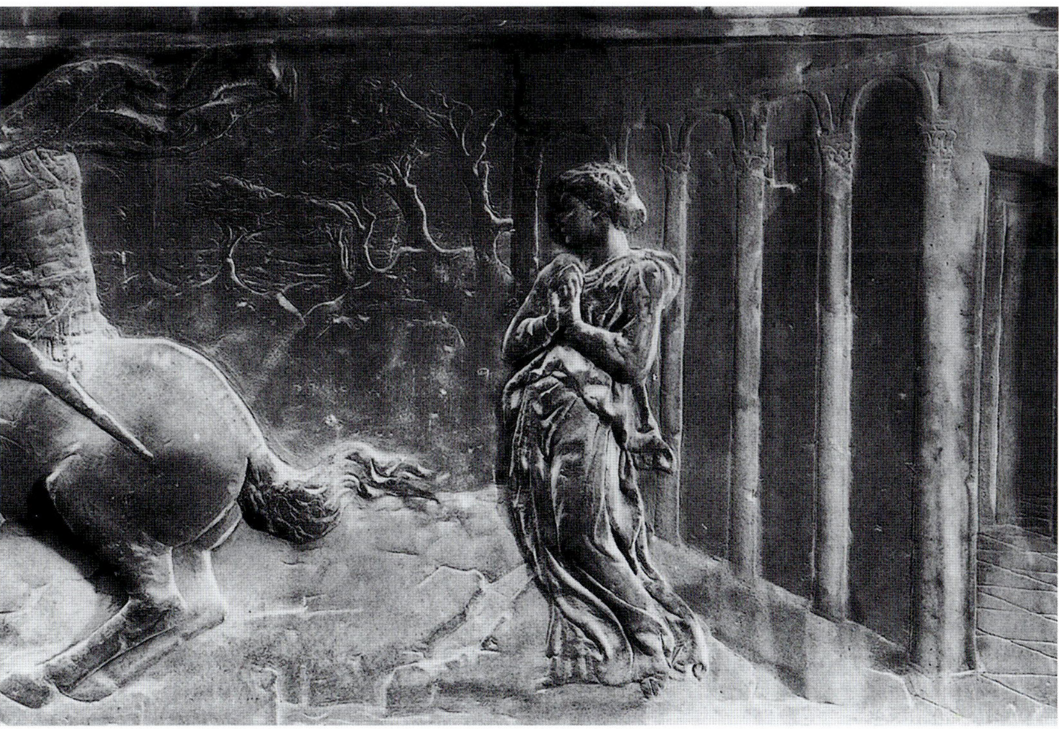

Facing page:
St George
by Donatello,
sculpted for
Orsanmichele,
now in the Bargello
Museum, Florence,
1416-1417.

Right:
*St George freeing
the princess*, detail
of the predella
sculpted by Donatello
for the *St George*,
now in the Bargello,
1416-1417.

The portico behind
the female figure
is the first artistic
application of
Brunelleschi's
principles of
perspective
construction.
Other particularly
significant aspects
of the work are the
typical very low relief
("schiacciato",
squashed), which
precisely because of
that achieves almost
pictorial effects, and
the treatment of the
drapery of the figures
which perfectly
explains why artists
studied its effects,
as Vasari recounts:
"make models in clay
and put soft cloths
on them, with an
infinity of creases,
to go back to them
and use them".

bly, as also in the case of Brunelleschi, the father's family hoped to make another notary of the heir of a son who had died young. To put it in the graceful prose of Antonio Manetti, Brunelleschi's biographer: "At a tender age, Filippo learned to read and to write and the abacus, as is customary for men of standing and for the better part in Florence, and so some letters, because his father was a notary and may have thought of making him do the same, because, to those who did not expect to be a doctor or notary or priest, few there were in that time who gave themselves or were given to letters". Again in the case of Masaccio, as in that of Brunelleschi, it will have been the personal bent of the individual that turned his life-choices elsewhere. So since the connections between families in the notarial milieu were close in those days, it might have been this circle that took in Masaccio on his arrival in Florence, helping him get into the workshops of paper-makers and illuminators in the areas of the Badia Fiorentina and Sant'Apollinare. And it is precisely in the Badia church that Vasari records there being a work by Masaccio, a fresco of *St Yves of Brittany with his pupils*, from the mention of which further clues can be gathered for the painter's launch in notarial circles: the building stood directly in front of the quarters of the Arte dei Notai, of which St Yves of Brittany was patron saint; and orphans were called "pupils" at the time. What could be more fitting than to set to the profession an orphan of a member of the Guild itself!

If the *San Giovenale Triptych* was Masaccio's inaugural work, it is clear that in the brief span of time that separates it from the later production some event or acquaintance of extreme importance must have occurred to explain the sudden flowering from a debut certainly promising, but still largely to be developed. Something that cannot be justified without a sort of "discipleship" with Brunelleschi. There is considerable evidence for the very close acquaintance between the two from early on, beginning with the *Libro di Antonio Billi* which, with great narrative efficacy, says of Masaccio: "He was loved by Filippo di ser Brunellesco, the great architect, because he saw him as of perspicacious intelligence, and he taught him many things of the trade". Brunelleschi's willingness to teach his discoveries to others is also witnessed to by Manetti, who reports that he "willingly taught those who seemed to want it and were apt to receive it". A view taken up also by Vasari who tells us that "he paid much attention to perspective... and he taught it particularly to Masaccio, then a young painter, a great friend of his".

This relationship is thus the keystone in any explanation of an artistic leap to maturity that has nothing developmental about it, indeed presents all the signs of a lightning-bolt. Certainly the stunning fresco of the *Trinity* in the church of Santa Maria Novella, of disputed date, could already be interpreted in this key: no one has never doubted his firm reliance on Brunelleschi, but a careful scrutiny of the technical characteristics along with a reconsideration of the creative genesis can lead one to consider it a very early work. From a technical point of view, in fact, the execution of the *Trinity* shows sparing use of "bianco di San Giovanni" (lime-white), a pigment very difficult to employ in fresco, that demands a consummate skill to master it. Masaccio resorted instead to the expedient of exploiting the white colour of the plaster in transparence, according to a method typical of the beginner in fresco.

In the reconstruction of the genesis of the work an interpretation of the relation between Brunelleschi and Masaccio can furthermore be made out and, more in general, of that between conception and realisation. The complexity of the illusionist construction of a chapel that "breaks through" the wall, the first complete application in painting of Brunelleschi's theory, of course needed an accurate preliminary study, which is almost unanimously attributed to the great architect. But what turns out to be particularly interesting is that the study also concerns the way of transposing onto the plaster the complex image designed on the drawing board. The display of methods of the genre – the snapped line, incisions, pouncing, squaring – some of which encountered here for the first time, each applied to conceptually different parts of the composition, can be interpreted as a demonstration of at least three principles, diverse but fitting perfectly together. First of all, the originating of the perspective construction is the work of someone other than the artist who paints it, who thus needs to refer to a

San Giovenale Triptych, detail, 1422. Cascia di Reggello, church of San Pietro.

The *Triptych* is also known for a subtle particularity hidden in the Virgin's halo. Normally gold-leaf decoration engraved with the burin was limited to decorative motifs, sometimes including religious symbols. Here instead the Madonna's halo has some written letters that at first sight might seem Arabic, but are employed for cryptic purposes to hide the theological definition: IHESUS CHRISTUS VIA VERITAS ET VITA. Why Masaccio chose to do so is still not explained, though it contributes to making the painting and its history even more interesting.

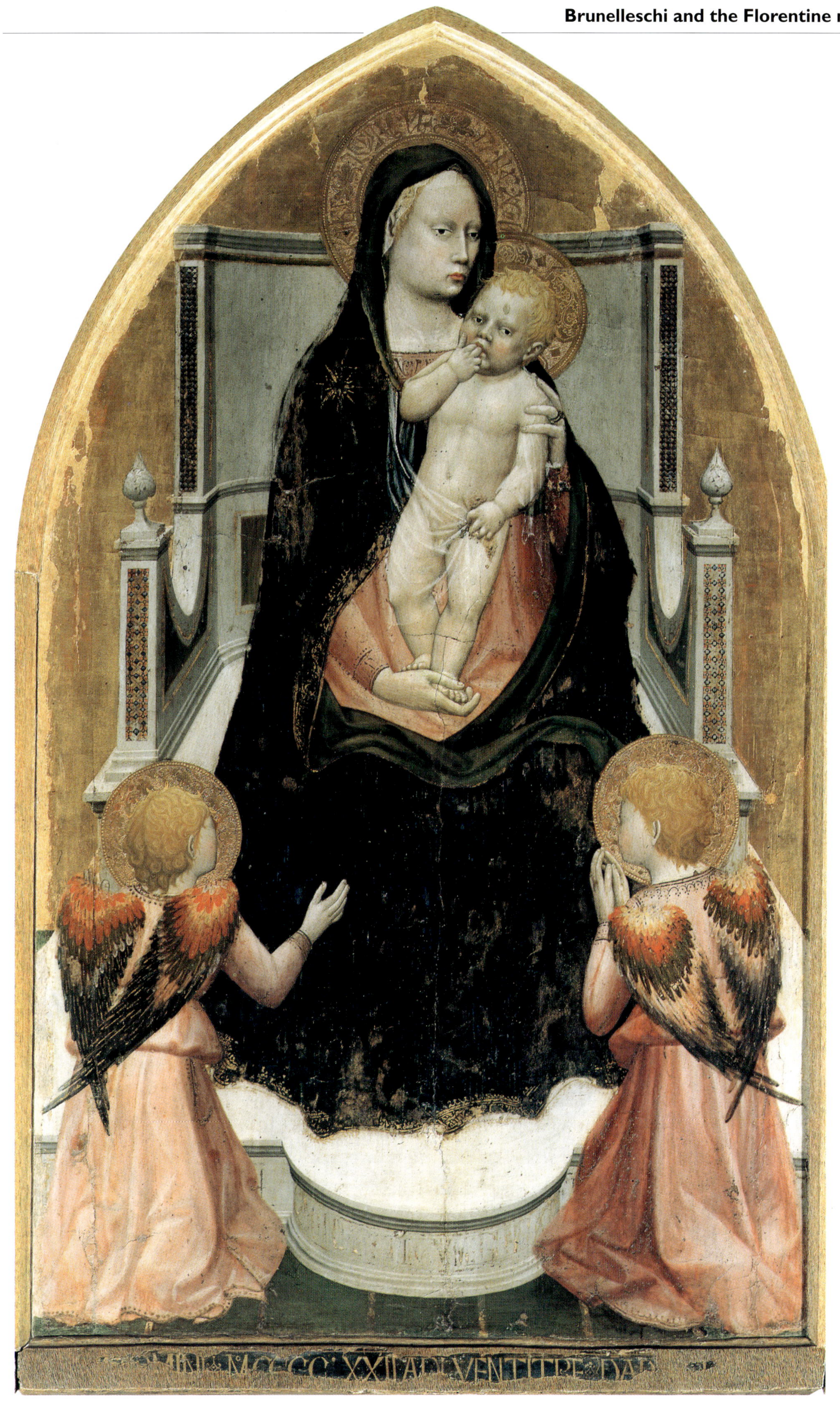

prototype (a design on paper) in an almost obsessive way. In second place, the artist is new to wall painting and must therefore employ many means to ensure an exact enlargement of the model (see the multiple and different squaring of the bust and face of the Madonna). Finally, Brunelleschi's tutoring come out in an assiduous way in the preparatory stage and in the

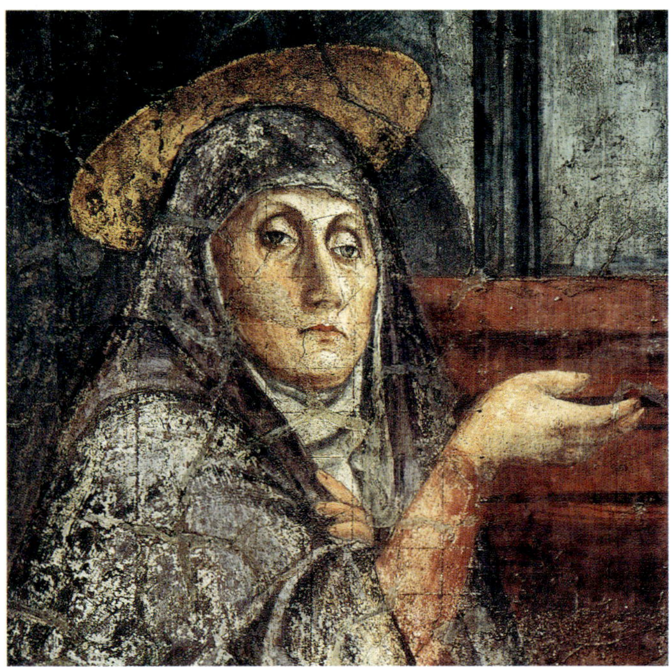 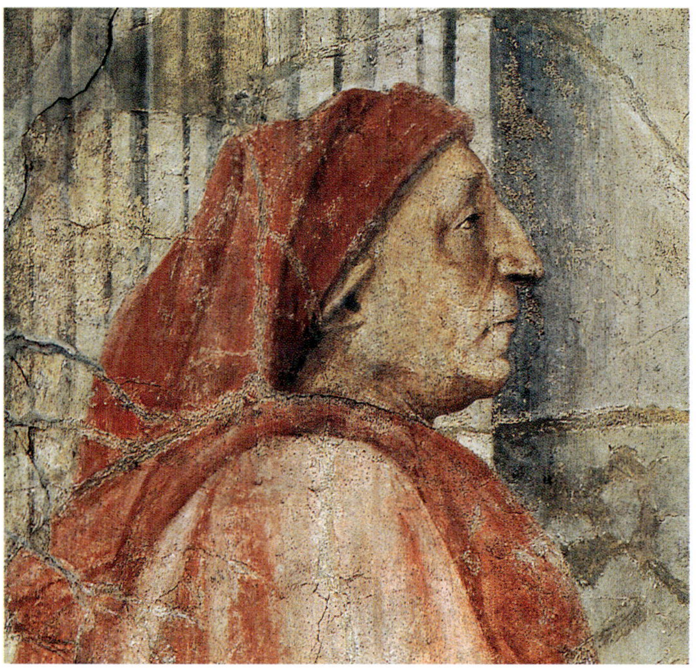

Trinity, details,
c. 1424. Florence,
Santa Maria Novella.

The figure of the Virgin seems to have been transposed to the wall from a preparatory drawing done in the studio and enlarged by squaring. The mesh thickens in relation to the face, evidently in order to study the details better.

first half of the stage of transposing onto the wall (left side), while the second part demands much less work of transposition, almost exclusively exploiting the specularity of the architecture. But also as regards the painting, with the passage of the days, the artist seems to acquire the techniques specific to mural painting and abandons almost all the maniacal transposition of the reference model.

We are looking almost at a propaedeutic moment: Masaccio has barely come out of Brunelleschi's school and is laying down the premises for a subsequent re-working that will lead him to a more pictorial interpretation of the geometric modules of the great architect. A moment of passage between the inadequate spatial rendering, Lorenzettian in origin, of the *San Giovenale Triptych* and the later results of the Brancacci and of the *Pisa Polyptych*; a beginning, therefore, and not a point of arrival. A moment which, even by re-interpreting the chronology of Brunelleschi, can only be set before 1426. On the 4th of February of that year, in fact, the architect was given the *de facto* direction of the works for the dome: Brunelleschi had to devote himself totally to the immense challenge and it seems improbable that in that urgent situation he could have found a way of teaching the young Masaccio the "breaking through" perspective of the *Trinity* except by drawing it for him, at least in the first stage.

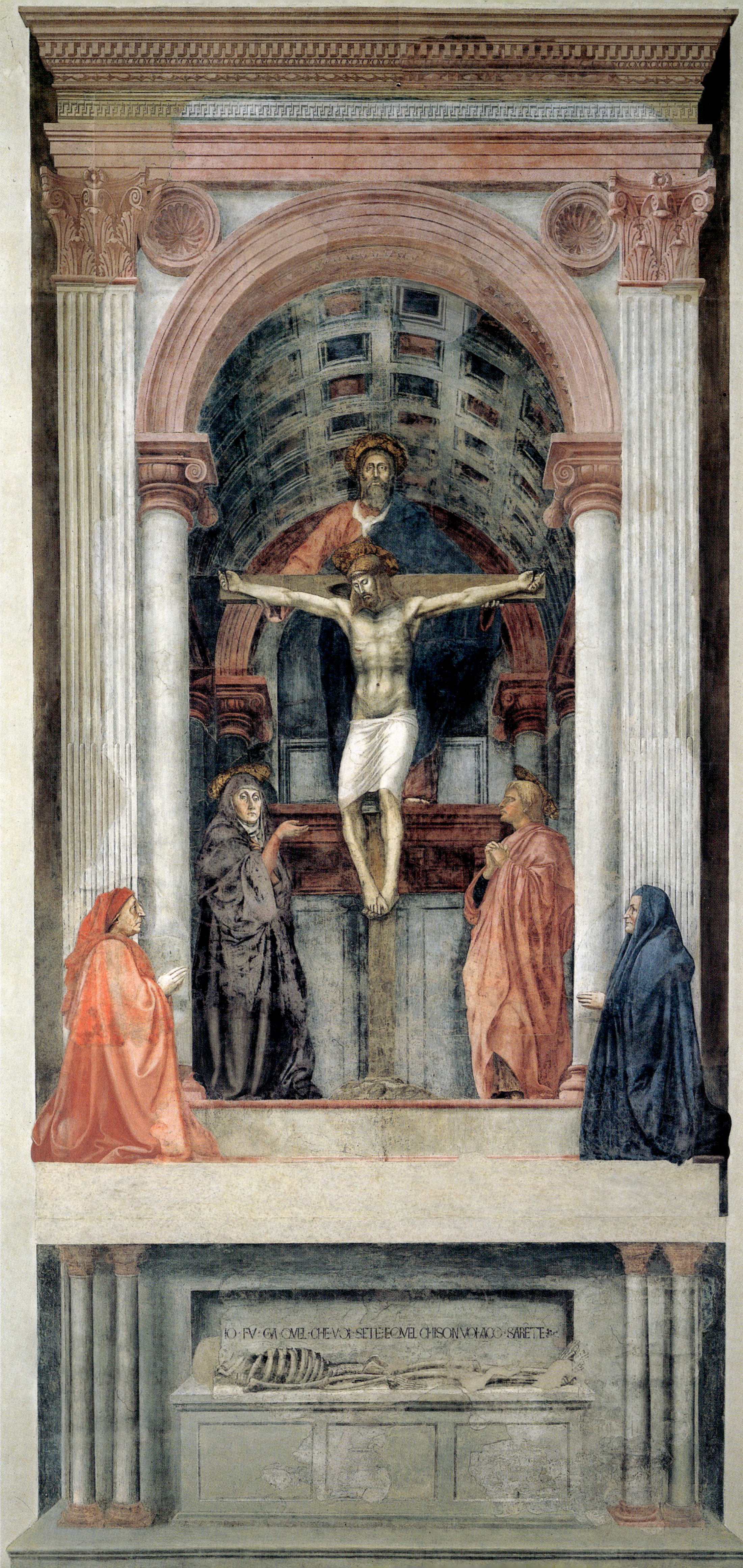

Trinity, c. 1424.
Florence, Santa Maria
Novella.

The representation
of the Trinity
was perhaps only
occasionally linked to
private commissions,
and was in any case
very close, because
of iconological
choices, to the
Dominican Order: a
solemn reconfirmation
of the ideas
of Scholasticism
and Thomism at
a time when they
were beginning
to be questioned
by Humanism.
The off-centre placing
of the fresco made
more intense the
involvement of the
faithful who came
into church by
the door from the
little Avelli cloister,
capturing their
attention through
the impact of the
trompe-l'oeil realism
of the building.

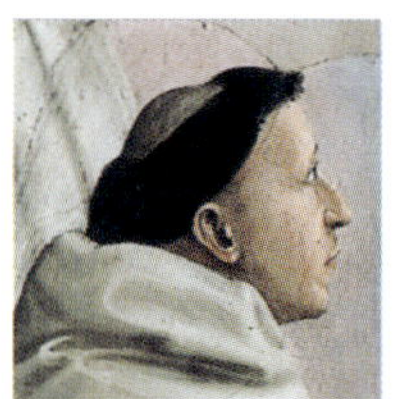

The collaboration
with Masolino

About a year after his debut marked by the *San Giovenale Triptych*, around 1423, Masaccio began his fortunate and in many ways mysterious collaboration with Masolino. The latter was a much older artist than Masaccio; born around 1388, he belonged to the previous generation. Of Florentine family or in any case a long-time resident of Florence, Tommaso di Cristofano di Fino was often called "da Panicale", giving an indication of his origins which, however, cannot be matched in the contemporary documents. Since there is a place in Valdarno called Panicale, not far from San Giovanni, many have believed since Vasari's time that the reason for the association between the two artists lay in their shared origins. But Vasari himself may have invented a legend that has no exact documentary backing.

Indeed Masolino goes without mention in Florentine documents up to September 1422, when he rents a house in the city. Many indications lead one to think not of a loss of pre-existent documentation but of a prolonged absence from Florence up to that date. First of all the fact that he, though adult, is always referred to in the documents as being in paternal care, something understandable if he needed someone to look after his interests in the city because of very long absence. Furthermore, though showing himself to be at that date a complete painter, Masolino was to enrol in the guild only in January 1423, three months after his return, as if to legitimise his position since he expected to be intensely and continuously active. It almost looks as if he came back to Florence because of precise demands for his work.

His familiarity with moving large distances is confirmed by later events, when, in mid 1425, in the very middle of intense work, Masolino accepted an offer to go to Hungary, then not quite next door for Florentines, which entailed a stay of all of three years. Furthermore, on the death of Pippo Spano, his Hungarian employer, in December 1426, Masolino's return destination was by no means Florence, a city substantially foreign to him,

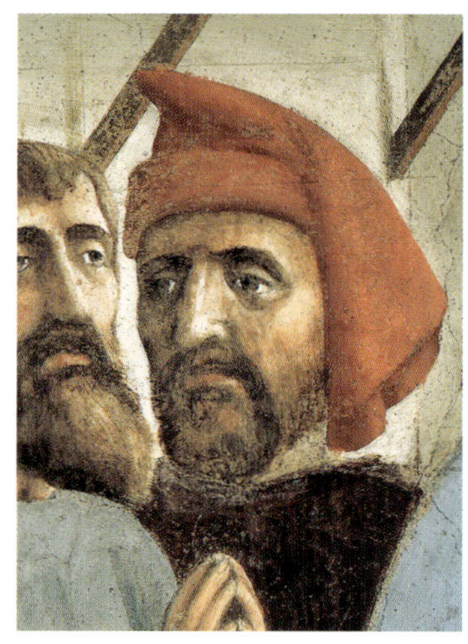

St Peter healing the sick with his shadow, detail with the presumed portrait of Masolino, c. 1424-1426. Florence, Brancacci Chapel.

Facing page:
The healing of the lame and the resurrection of Tabitha by Masaccio and Masolino, detail, c. 1424-1426. Florence, Brancacci Chapel.

but very likely Rome. He seems to have returned to Florence only later to sell all his property, freeing himself finally from his father and setting off for other destinations, heading first for Rome and then Castiglione Olona and Lombardy, where we lose track of him.

Given this fragmentary biography it is difficult to make a credible reconstruction of Masolino's beginnings and his artistic training: Vasari first calls him "rinettatore" of the doors of the baptistery on Ghiberti's site and then pupil of Starnina. But Vasari's notion was put in doubt time ago by the fact that in the Florence of the time there was a man with the same name as the painter, another Tommaso di Cristofano who followed the trade of goldsmith, and was therefore more fitted to be Ghiberti's assistant.

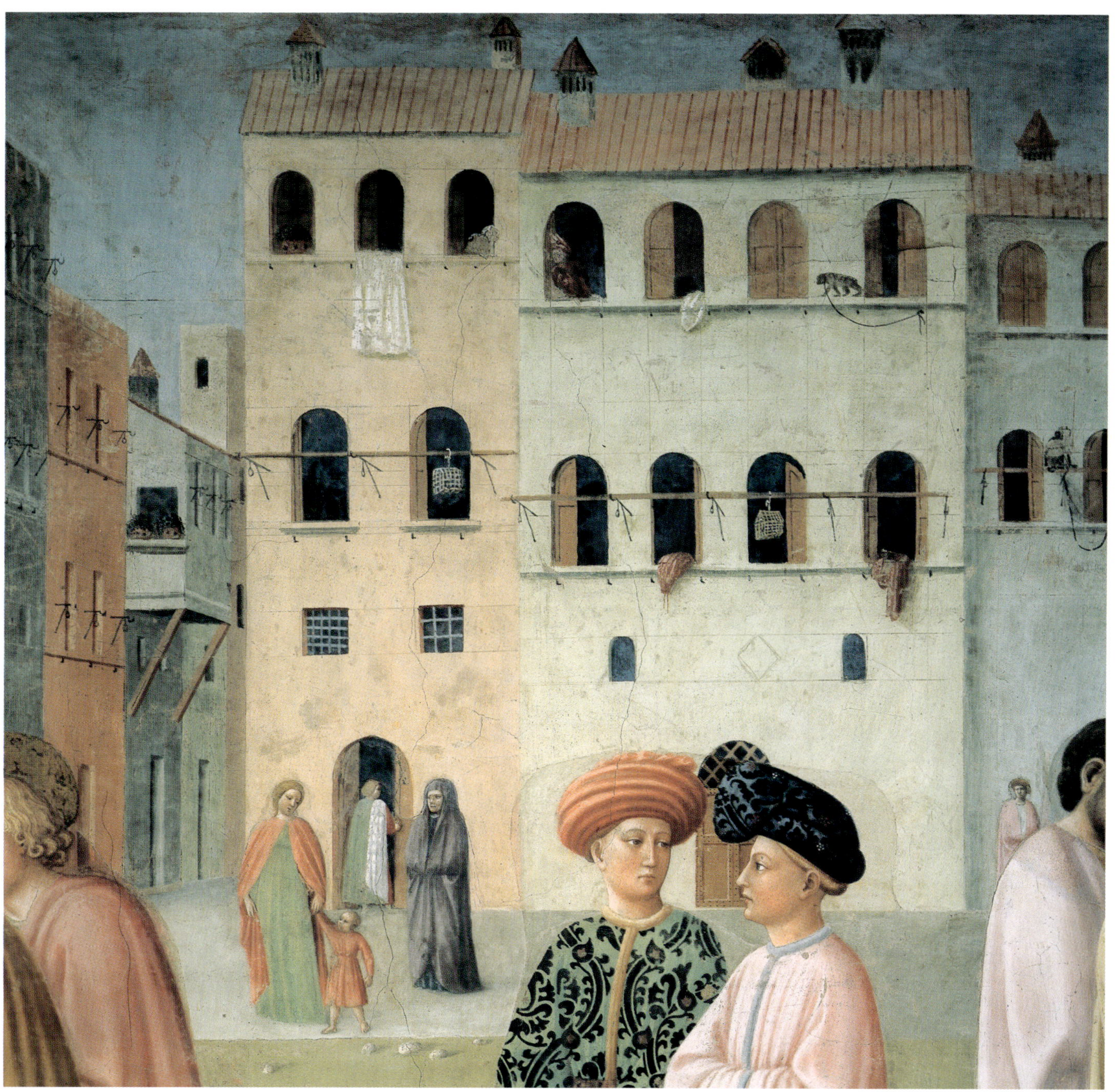

It is of some interest, instead, to consider the fact that in legal and fiscal documents Masolino's father describes himself as "imbiancatore". In the sphere of the painting trade in fifteenth-century Florence the work of "room painter" was one of the minor activities; many of those engaged in the trade were enrolled in the Arte dei Medici e Speziali. Apprenticeship in the family business may have been the first and most logical school for Masolino, as was the case with many other artists of the period. If we consider the silence of the documents on Masolino up to 1422 and the equally mysterious silence about his father, one might suggest that their absence from Florence was due to long roaming together in search of work, following the market and accepting employment where it was offered.

The specific technical competence of Masolino, for that matter, seems to have been, at least at the beginning, that of the fresco. Perhaps it was precisely because of important and well-paid commissions, like that of the Compagnia della Croce in Santo Stefano degli Agostiniani in Empoli, finished in 1424, that Masolino returned to Florence. The commission for the Brancacci may well have been his, at least initially; and then, when the period of collaboration with Masaccio closed, Masolino went back to being mainly a fresco painter. Painting in fresco made it possible, at the limit, not to have a proper workshop, but to exercise a sort of itinerant trade, setting up shop on each new occasion and finding manpower *in situ*. This could explain how Masolino could exercise his trade even with prolonged (or continuous) periods away from Florence. And could also provide reasons for his technique of painting that reveals methods foreign to the Florentine milieu.

We know nothing for certain about the occasion that gave rise to the collaboration between Masaccio and Masolino, a true financial and work partnership, a "compagnia", as it was called at the time, regulated according to the laws of the time. There are no plausible suggestions to be based on the whereabouts of the dwellings of the two artists in the period prior to their collaboration. It should, however, be remembered that Florence numbered less than 40,000 inhabitants at the time and that one of the points in setting up the Arte dei Medici e Speziali was that of creating close ties among the people enrolled, not least for reason of mutual checks. Even without seeking specific occasions, the meeting of members of the same trade must not have been impossible. There is, however, a more specific suggestion, i.e. that the occasion of encounter was the commission from the Carnesecchi, the family of Florentine grandees that had property and possessions in the countryside around San Giovenale, one of whose members commissioned from Masolino the *Madonna of Humility* (now in Bremen) in 1423, as can be seen from arms on the frame.

Madonna of Humility done by Masolino for the Carnesecchi and the Boni family, now in the Kunsthalle of Bremen, 1423.

St Julian, painted by Masolino for the *Carnesecchi Triptych* and kept in the Cestello Archiepiscopal Museum, Florence, c. 1423-1424.

Masolino's figures are characterised by a particular late Gothic elegance: the short transparent vest of the Child in the Bremen painting, his kicking in the Virgin's arms, St Julian's rich fur-lined cloak, the clothes in red lacquer on silver-leaf are exquisite formal and material features that hark back to a courtly world by then on the wane.

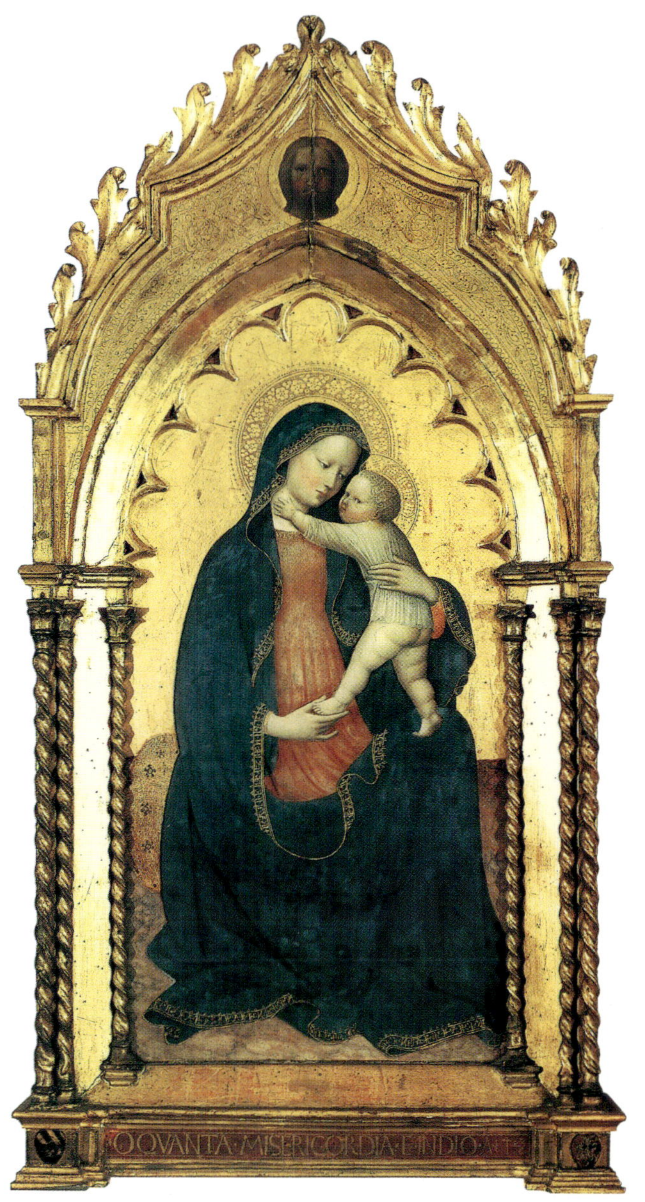

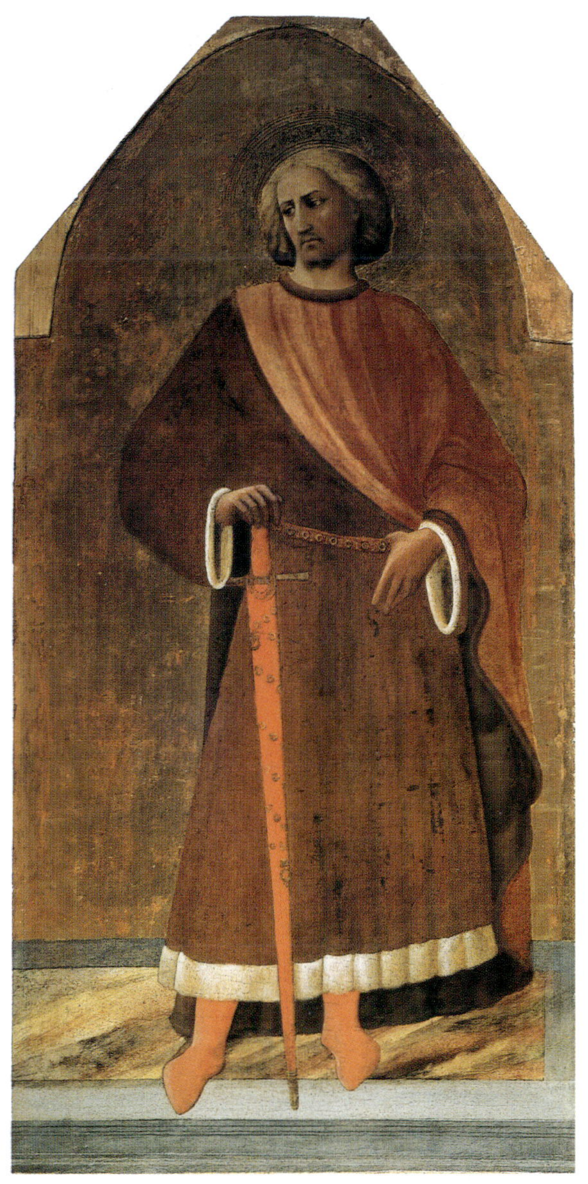

The Carnesecchi commissioned the *Triptych* for their chapel in Santa Maria Maggiore in Florence, the first work of collaboration between the two artists. A collaboration begun presumably after March 1424, when Masolino broke his partnership with the painter Francesco d'Antonio, with whom he is often mentioned in records between 1422 and 1424. The *Triptych*, largely lost as the result of the seventeenth-century renewal of the church in which it was kept, is described by Vasari, who speaks of "a chapel beside the side door that leads to San Giovanni, where there is the panel and altarpiece by Masaccio": a chapel dedicated to St Catherine of Alexandria, frescoed by Paolo Uccello. In the main register of the *Triptych* were painted "an Our Lady, Saint Catherine and Saint Julian, and on the predella he did some small figures of the life of Saint Catherine and Saint Julian killing his father and mother; and in the middle he did the Nativity of Jesus Christ, with that simplicity and vividness that was his own in working". Of the whole complex we now have only the *St Julian* and the predella with the vi-

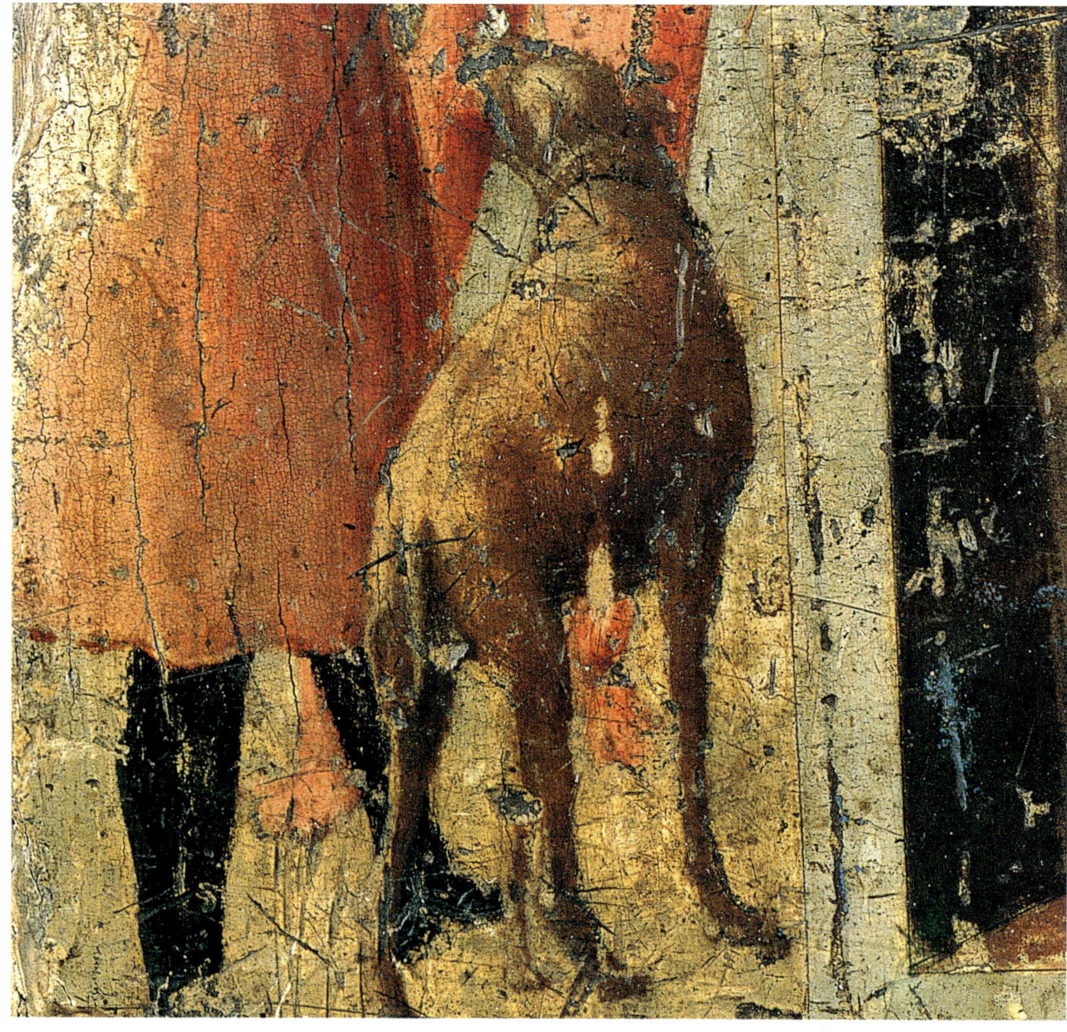

Scenes from the legend of St Julian, detail, c. 1423-1424. Florence, Horne Museum.

The depiction of the dog in this small scene is of extraordinary and modern naturalism. With marvellous compactness its incredible foreshortening gives spatial definition to the scene. Its inclusion also has an important narrative significance: just back from hunting, St Julian meets the devil and falls into his trap. Only his hound, symbol of fidelity, shows it has sniffed out the dangerous nature of the being who comes towards them and who tempts man precisely on the issue of fidelity.

olent story connected to him. The central panel, the *Madonna and Child*, survived until 1923, when it was stolen from the church on the outskirts of Florence where it was kept. There has been no trace of it since.

As if to compensate for the loss of the greater part of the panels, two predella sections with the story of St Julian compete for the honour of belonging to the *Carnesecchi Triptych*. And what makes the contest more intriguing is the fact that one is by Masaccio and the other by Masolino. Nothing could better exemplify the difference between the two artists. Masolino chose a narrative formula that centred on the drama as it is happening, with the *grand-guignol* killing of the unwitting parents in bed. Masaccio entrusted the pathos to the moment when the guilty Julian realises, in meeting his wife, the tragic error that jealousy has forced him into. Here there is a scene that, though irremediably scratched, is a powerful anticipation of the *Expulsion* in the Brancacci Chapel, with the guilty man's mute cry to heaven, conscious of being unable to go back in time and make good the crime committed. And again Masaccio chose, unlike Masolino, to simplify the characters' garments, not to stress St Julian's belonging to the knightly order through the elegance of garments lined with fur. But the insertion of the dog

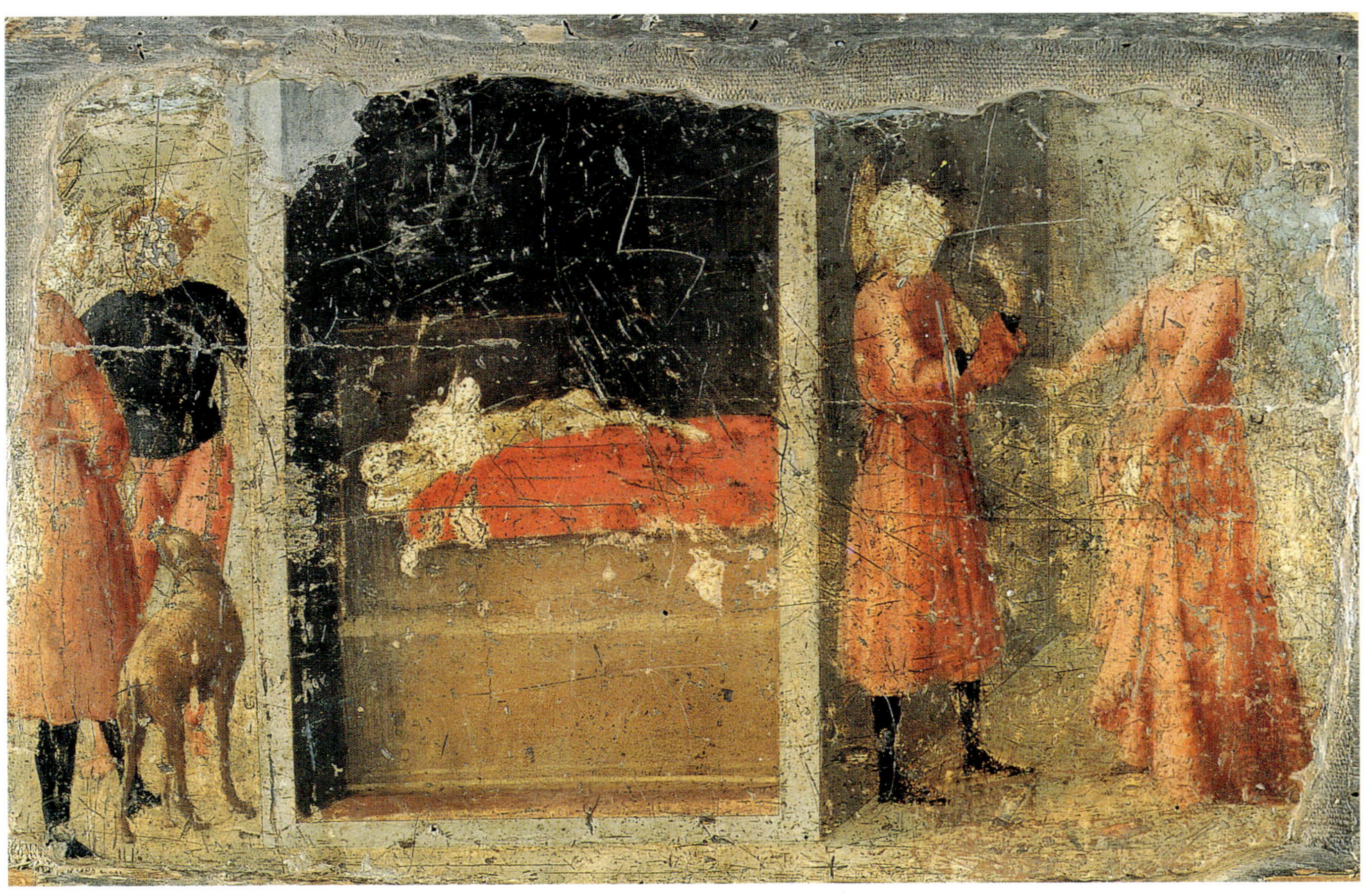

Scenes from the legend of St Julian, c. 1423-1424. Florence, Horne Museum.

is marvellous, the second in the portrayal of small animals begun with the piglet at the feet of St Anthony in the *San Giovenale Triptych*. Particularly significant is the fact that Masaccio's predella has recently been proved to belong to the *Carnesecchi Triptych* on technical basis and hence the choices opted for by the two artists must have been all the more evident, when one considers that this altarpiece scene was matched by Masolino's full-length *St Julian*, a knight "from a Pre-Raphaelite dream" as Pietro Toesca described it at the moment of its rediscovery.

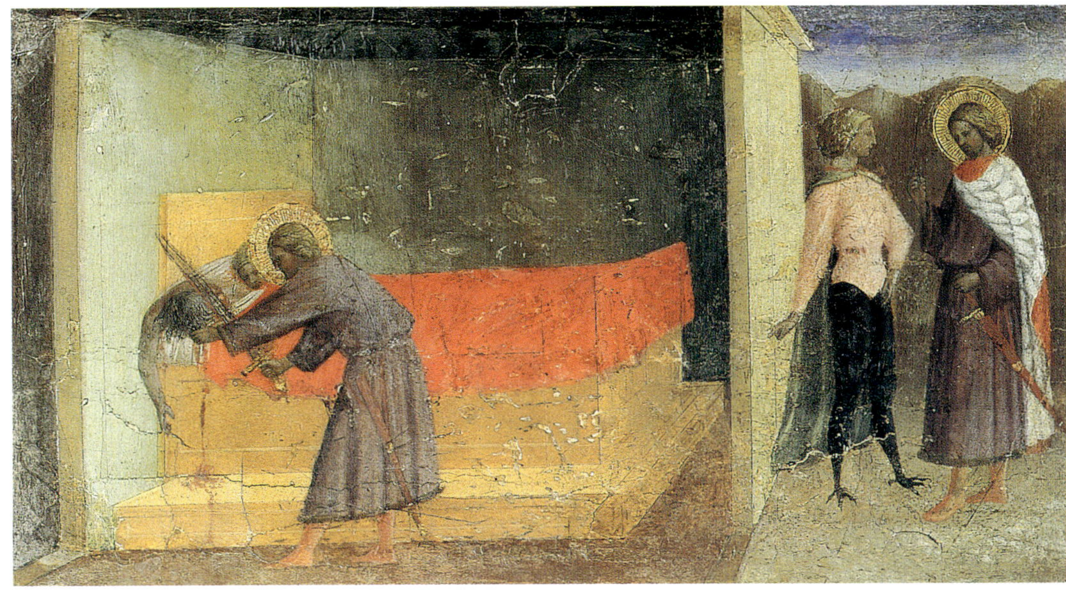

Scenes from the legend of St Julian, section of the predella done by Masolino, in the Musée Ingres in Montauban, c. 1425.

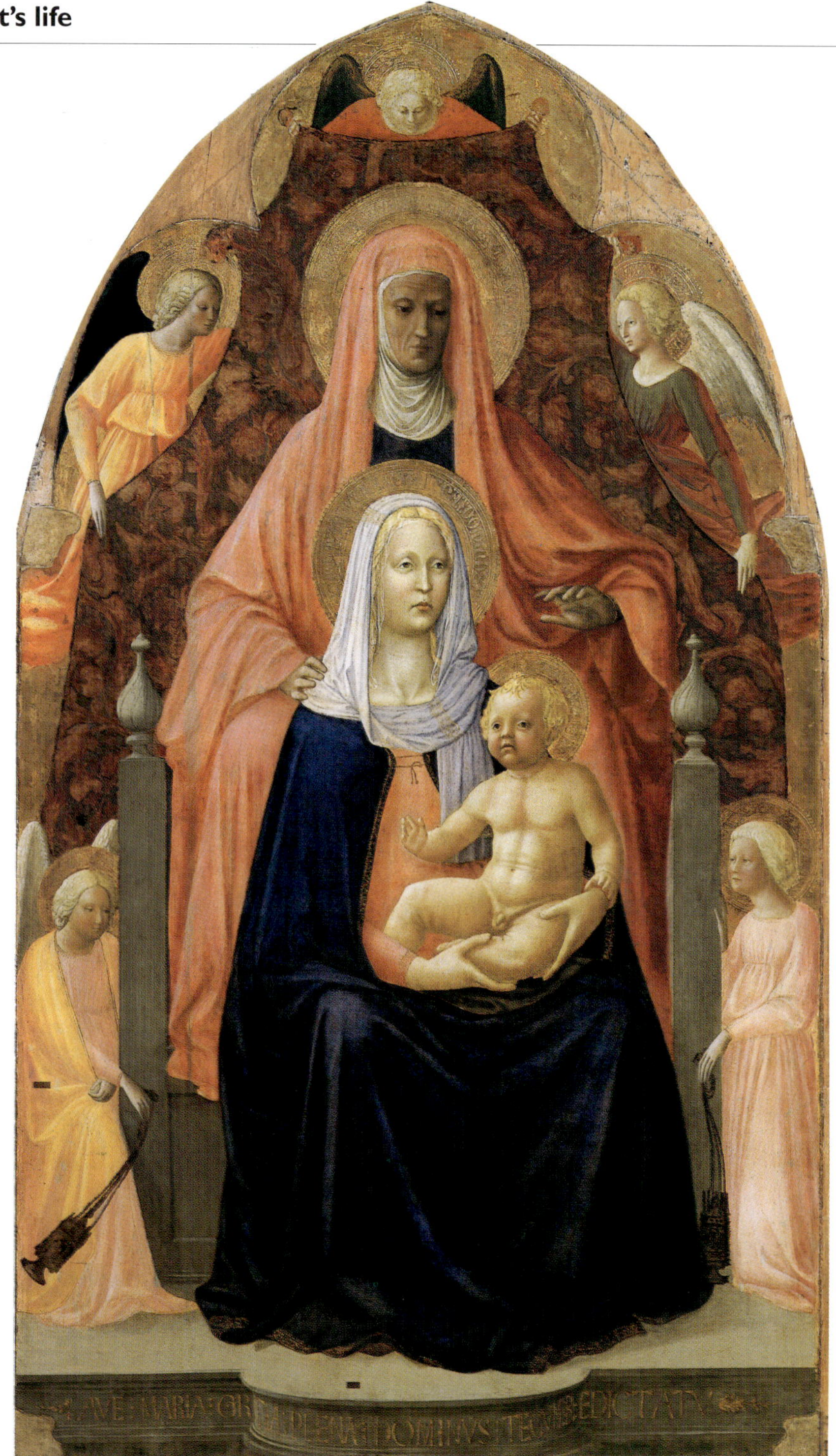

St Anne Metterza, done by Masaccio and Masolino, whole and detail, now in the Uffizi Gallery, c. 1424-1425.

On 26 July 1343 Gualtieri di Brienne, known as the Duke of Athens, the only tyrant in the century-long history of the Florentine republic, was driven out by a popular uprising. Whereon the Florentines began to venerate St Anne, the saint whose feast fell that day, elevated as guardian of the republican cause and of Florence itself. Later on the saint was often portrayed in an attitude of protection towards the city, which here seems symbolised by the Virgin, titular of the cathedral of Santa Maria del Fiore.

We do not know how Masaccio and Masolino shared out the remaining sections of the *Carnesecchi Triptych* (we only know from old photographs that the stolen *Madonna and Child* was unequivocally by Masolino), but it is probable that what to us today seem absolute differences and insuperable disequalities must not have seemed so at the time. To the extent that the two artists shortly afterwards took on together a much closer collaboration within the ambit of a single panel: the *St Anne Metterza* (Madonna and Child with St Anne as third) for the church of Sant'Ambrogio. For several decades now critical examination of the collaboration of Masaccio and Masolino in the making of this work has agreed on some fixed points and on a differentiated medley of minor hypotheses. Among the fixed

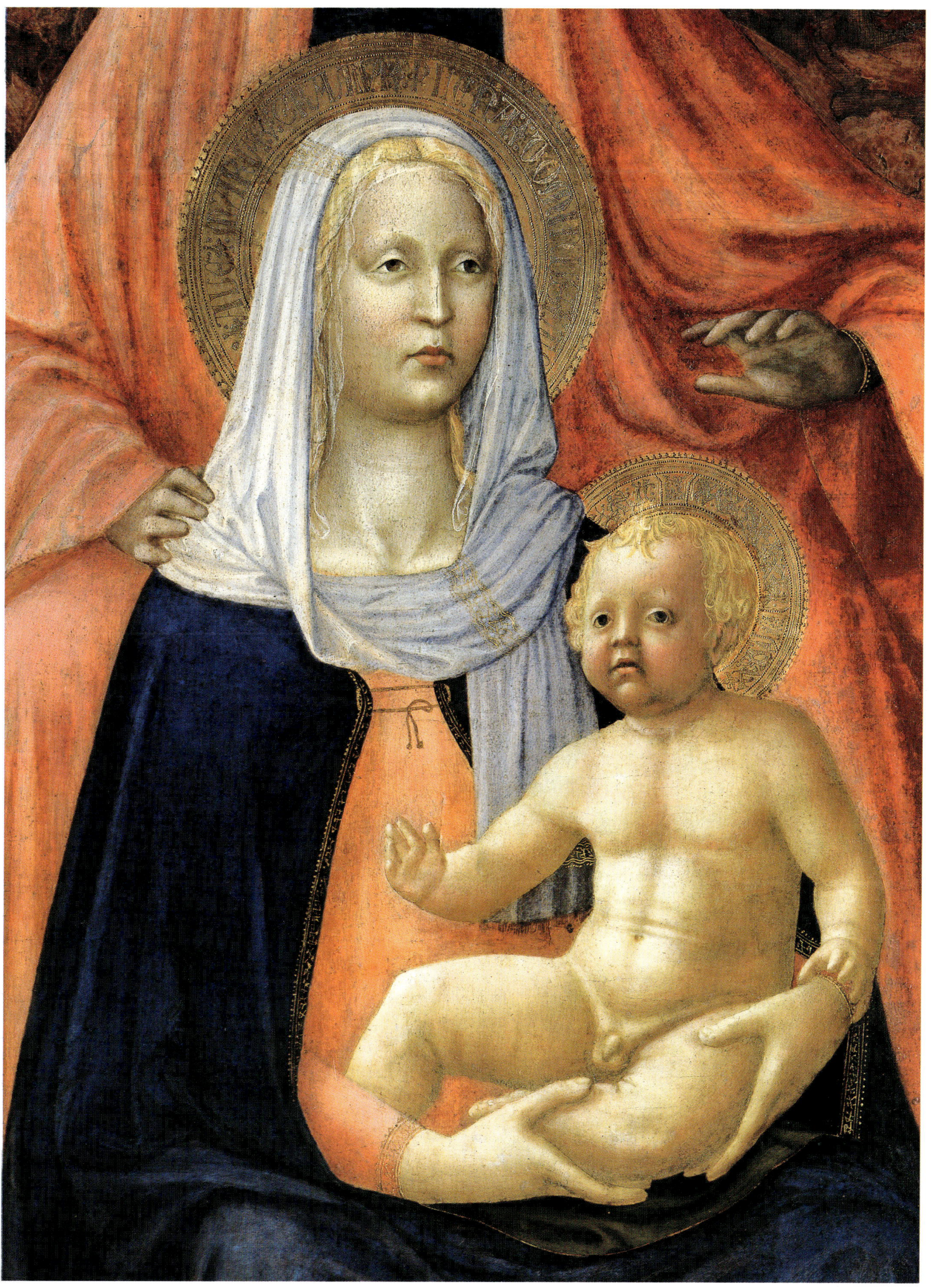

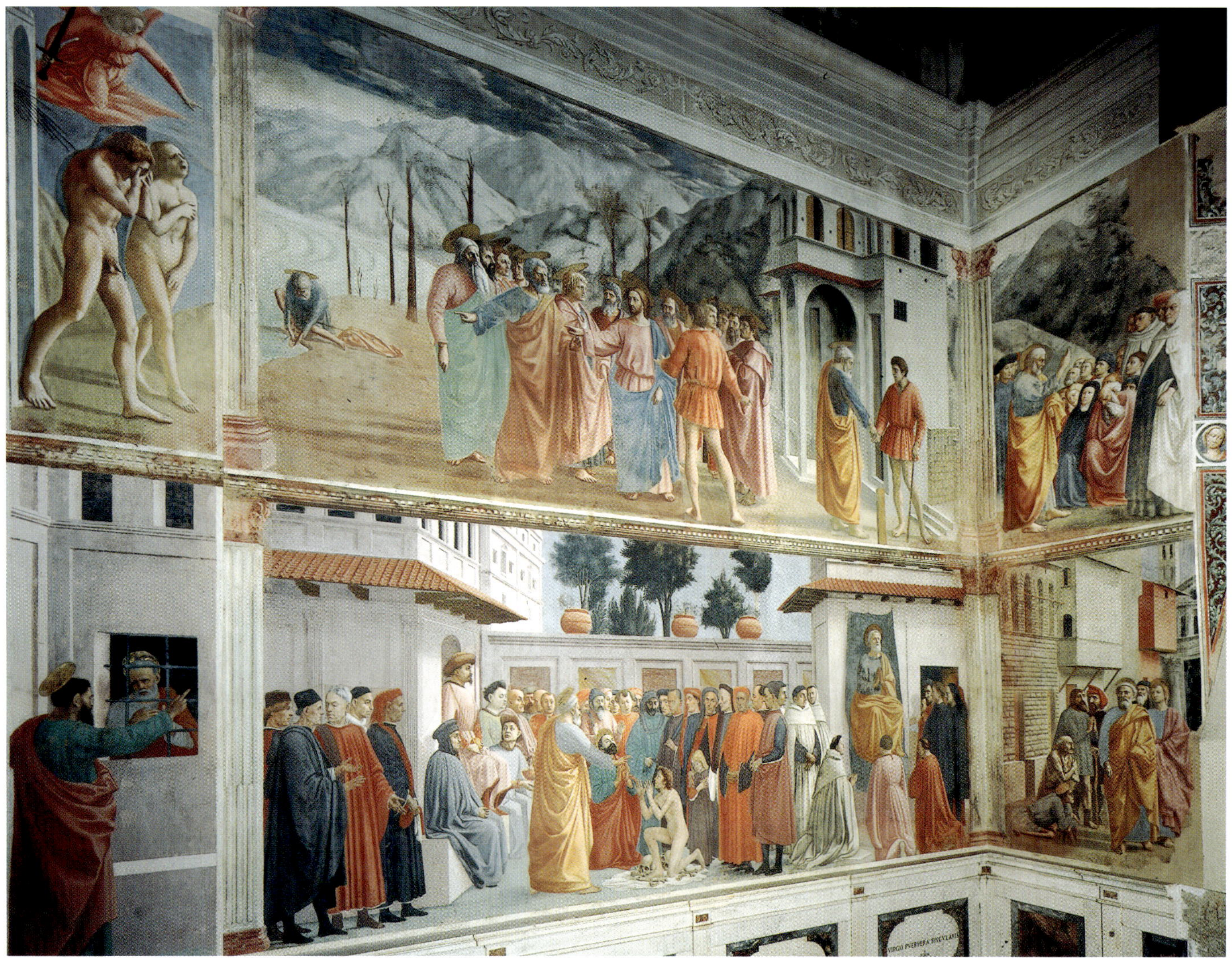

points stands the general attribution to Masaccio of the group of the Madonna with Child and of the angel holding the curtain on the right; to Masolino of St Anne and the two other two flying angel. While consensus is less general on who was responsible for the two (without doubt stylistically weaker) angels with thurible, "tired with being pink", in Longhi's felicitous description, for the general conception of the composition, for the chronological succession and logic of execution. To all this is often added the sparse knowledge of artistic techniques that leads to make suggestions impossible in terms of materials, like that of Masolino breaking off in the painting phase and the taking over by Masaccio with consequent change of part of the composition. A break and a restart, within a work done in the painting technique of *St Anne Metterza*, is absolutely out of the question: the gesso used in preparation, in fact, to which Cennini devoted many accurate prescriptions both of working it and preserving it, is an extremely delicate material, in the physico-morphological perfection of which lies much of the secret of successful tempera painting. The surface of the gesso, finely worked so as to give it notable characteristics of smoothness and

The Brancacci Chapel in the church of Santa Maria del Carmine in Florence, frescoed by Masaccio and Masolino between 1424 and 1426 and finished by Filippino Lippi in 1481-1483.

Upper register, left wall: *The expulsion of Adam and Eve from Paradise*, *The tribute*, *The preaching of St Peter*; right wall: *The baptism of the neophytes*, *The healing of the lame and the resurrection of*

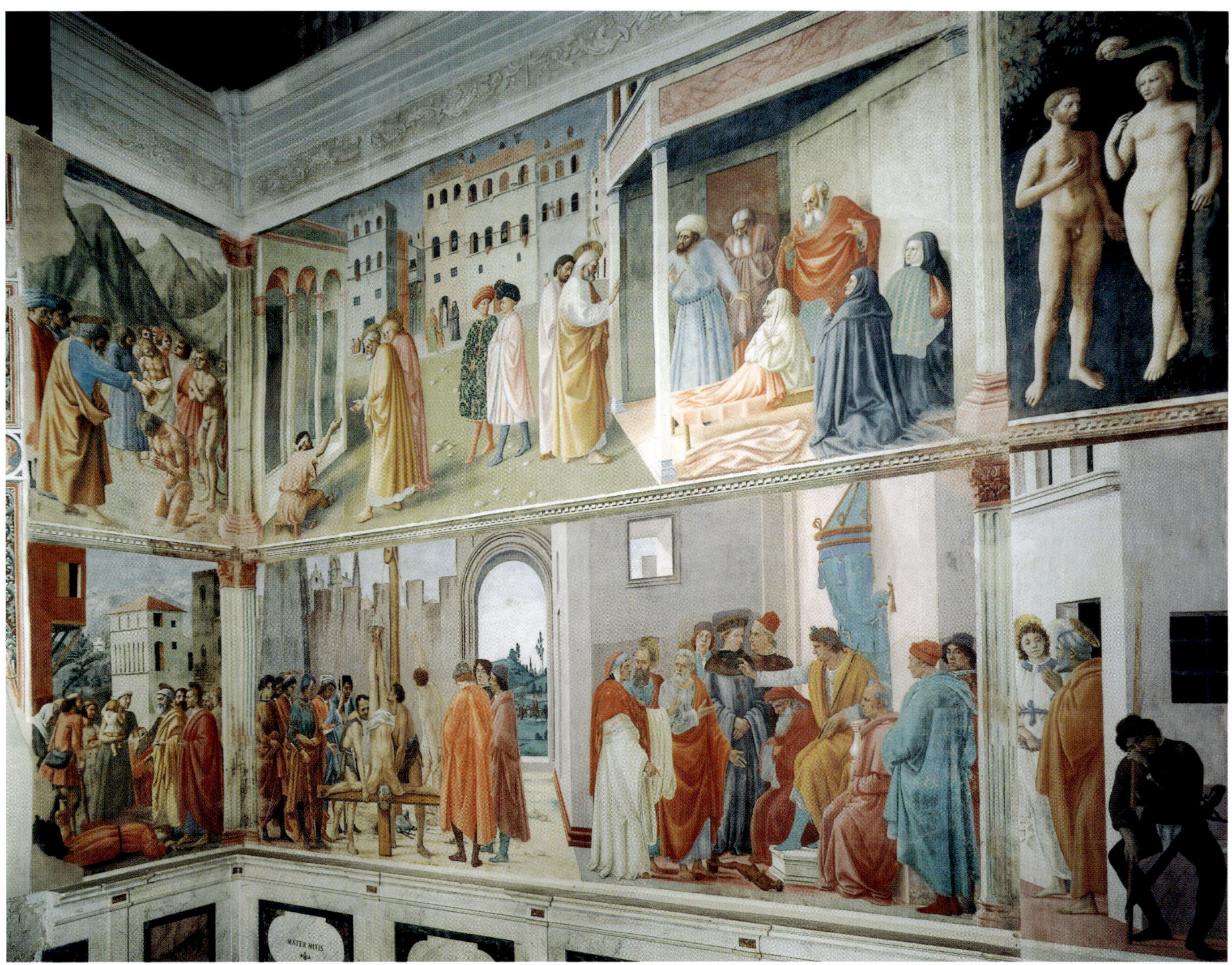

Tabitha, Temptation of Adam and Eve.
Lower register, left wall:
St Peter in prison visited by St Paul, The resurrection of the son of Theophilus and St Peter in cathedra, St Peter healing the sick with his shadow; right wall:
The bestowing of alms and the death of Ananias, The dispute of Simon Magus and the crucifixion of St Peter, The angel liberating St Peter from prison.

brilliance, if left too long without painting becomes rigid, rough, difficult to work except at the expense of the quality of the pictorial outcome. Long breaks in the course of work are therefore implausible. Faced with such a delicate surface, the prior planning of the image and of the composition had to be as careful as possible so as to avoid having to make corrections on the gesso. The stages in the general setting-out of the image required, as one of the first work operations, the use of incisions to guide the application of golden or silver leaves and absolute precision was needed at this stage since later correction was impossible without impairing the quality of the outcome. In the face of such a logical, sequential and pressing procedure in the work phases many notions about alternation and correction between the various hands may be ruled out. Masolino cannot have left the *St Anne Metterza* unfinished at the time of his departure for Hungary in 1425, as some people have suggested.

Apart from the reasons given above on the material composition of the painting, the suggestion goes against logical considerations relating to the small size of the piece and a journey that could not have been impromptu

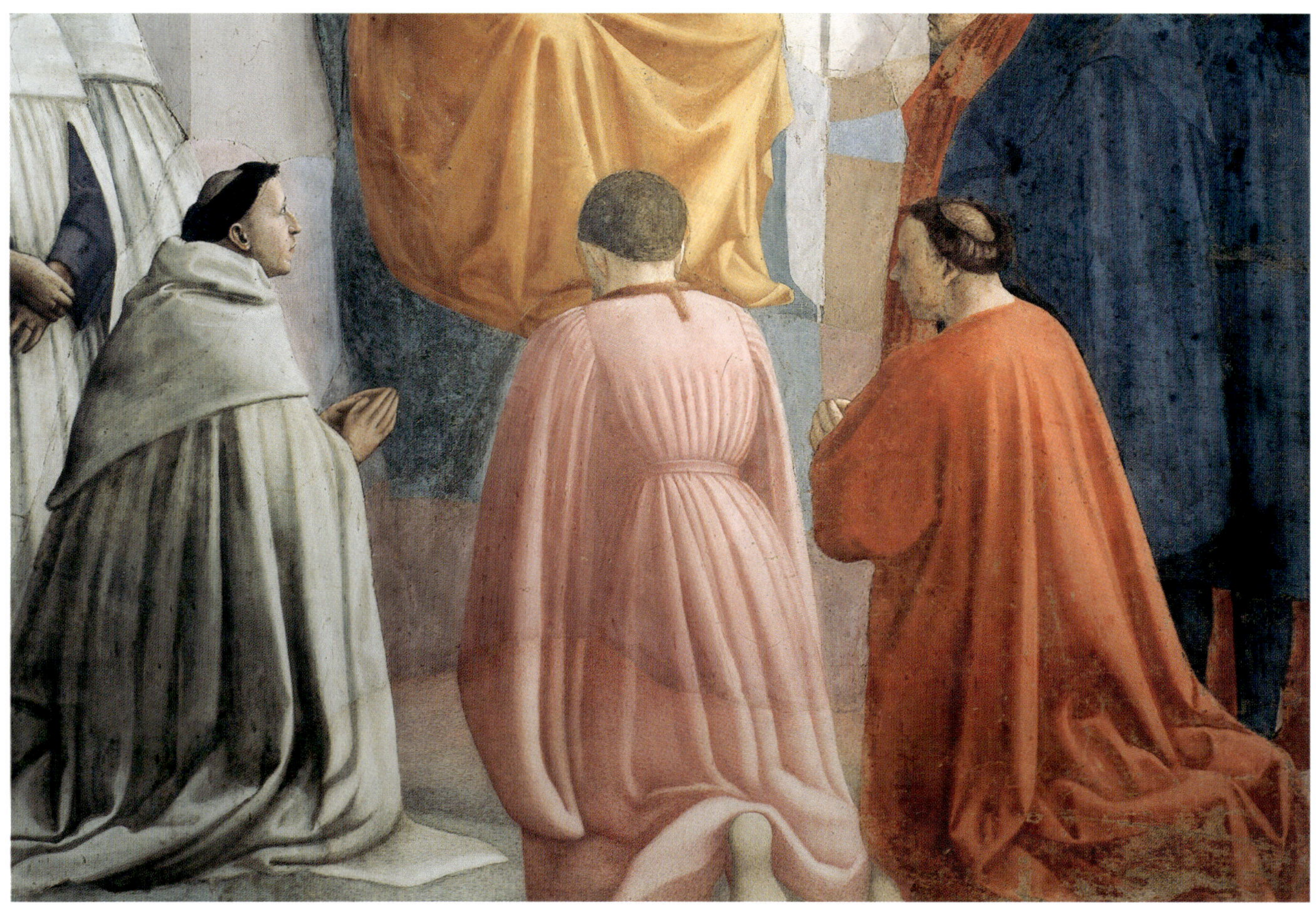

St Peter in cathedra, detail, c. 1424-1426. Florence, Brancacci Chapel.

Among the bystanders are probable portraits of some of the Carmelite friars more directly linked to the Brancacci cycle and in relations with Masaccio.

and impossible to delay but, given the time it would require and the distance to be covered, must have been properly planned in advance. Furthermore the conjectured modification by Masaccio of the prior conception of Masolino at the moment of his later intervention is not compatible with overall planning of the painting in the design stage.

Planning that had to be very precise given the great variety of metals used, if one thinks not only of the gold background, but above all of the great parade of honour behind the divine group, all done on leaves of worked silver and, let us remember, done before the laying on of colours. It is important to note at this point that the decoration of the cloth is achieved by a juxtaposition of pomegranate motifs on a thick squared mesh in the background, produced by incisions. The planning of the motif is almost perfect, with the cuts stopping exactly in correspondence to the flower clusters and fruit, showing therefore that the goldbeaters responsible for the mesh had been given very precise guidelines. The controlled nature of the execution undoubtedly had precise aesthetic goals (the idea of representing a counter-cut velvet brocade would have been impoverished in its effects if the additional elements – the pomegranate – had not been given an aspect of wholeness by sparing the ground from any incisions) and is as equally closely monitored in every other area of the painting.

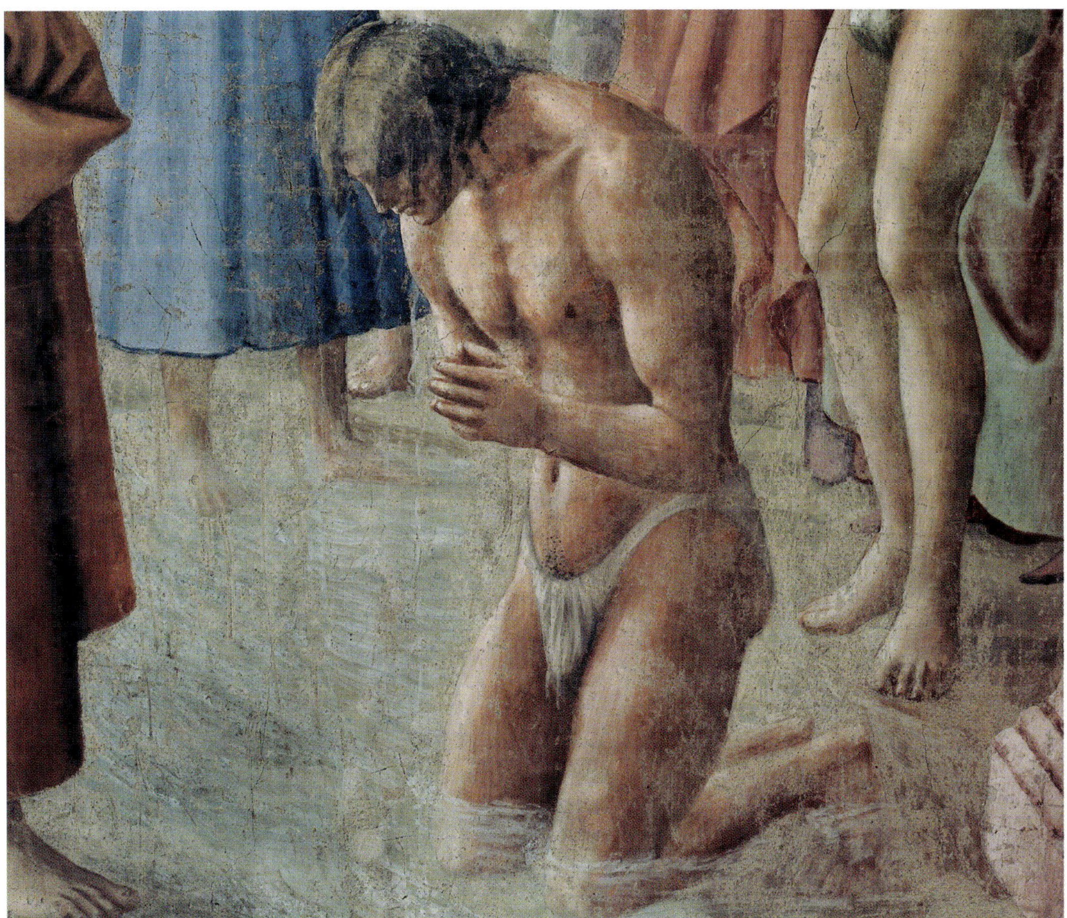

The baptism of the neophytes, detail, c. 1424-1426. Florence, Brancacci Chapel.

The figures of the catechumens, nude and cleansed with the sacred waters of Baptism, were a chance for Masaccio to get down to the study of rendering anatomy, something difficult to conceive of at the period outside the religious context. As Vasari also records, the artist "sought more than other masters to do nudes and foreshortened views of the figure, something little done before him".

So it remains fairly difficult to find a distinction of roles in this stage that would enable us to draw conclusions about the leading role of one or the other artist. Such tightly-knit participation and responsibility necessarily leads us to suggest a form of collaboration that could not be occasional but had to arise and grow in continuity and work sharing not only from the intellectual but also from the material standpoint.

If the *Carnesecchi Triptych* can be seen as a collaboration of the more traditional kind, in which each artist took a distinct section, the *St Anne Metterza* instead tells us of a relationship that has grown and ripened to the point of enabling synchronous working on a space of less than two square metres; including even possible minor collaborators, to whom are to be attributed the two angels with thurible.

The organisation of work in a workshop could be very different from what we seek to reconstruct *a posteriori* on the basis of stylistic readings and with a very different mind-set in the perception of art and work from that of the period in question. In a space as limited as the surface of this painting, it is not necessarily the case that one of the painters in the workshop reserved a specific area of the painting for himself and executed it in a totally independent way, from the design to finishing touches of paint. There were no strict demarcations of territory.

The progress of the work might follow chance criteria, physical presence in the workshop, greater ease or greater interest in executing certain phases rather than others. It is in this way, perhaps less lyrical and evocative, but certainly more in tune with the reality of a trade such as that of "craft working" in the Florence of the early fifteenth century, that the history of the frescoes in the Brancacci Chapel in the church of the Carmine in Florence should be read (pp. 48-55). A chapel still much debated in terms of the relationships between the private commission (from the Brancacci, a family of merchants involved in the political life of the Florentine republic) and the religious Order (the Carmelites, a mendicant Order less widespread and less studied than the Franciscans or the Dominicans but most important in the social life of the populous and busy quarter of Oltrarno fiorentino; an Order that, among other things, staged in its church the "sacred representations" in which Brunelleschi's prodigious machines took part). Frescoes that represent the stories of St Peter, the sub-text of none of which is entirely clear. They are still difficult to date and, in certain sections, of debatable attribution.

It has been suggested that the commission was possibly first given to Masolino, who then involved his younger companion. Yet Masaccio was perhaps the better candidate for the commission since he had already worked for the friars of the Carmine on the (lost) depiction of the consecration of the church itself in 1422. It was a mural in terra-verde highly praised by Vasari who describes how Masaccio "had known so well how to put on the level of that square, five and six in a row, the arrangement of those people who go decreasing with proportion and judgement, according to the sight of the eye… that natural people not do so well".

Overall the issue is far from clear, though Masolino and Masaccio worked together for a certain time side by side, up to September 1425. At that summer's end, while the work was going on busily, Masolino left Florence for Hungary. There commissions were awaiting him from Pippo Spano, i.e. Filippo Scolari, the rich Florentine who had become counsellor to the Emperor Sigismund and commander of his troops. This good fortune had earned him the title of Count of Timișoara and in Italy the nickname Spano (from the original Magyar for "governor").

According to contemporary sources, Scolari, a great patron and proponent of the arts, had had built in Hungary "around one hundred and eighty chapels from the foundations… up to final summit and to their perfection… the fair castle, and more churches made new, with many rich vestments and many other magnificences," summoning many Italian artists and, where possible, Florentine ones. In 1425, however, at the moment of

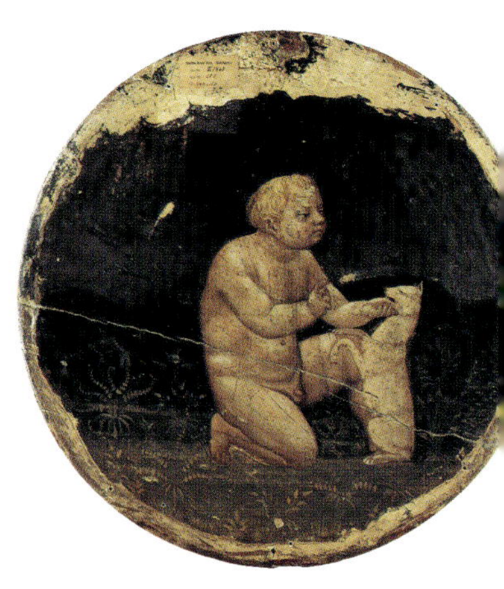

Birthing-stool, back with *Allegorical figure* (above) and *Nativity* (facing page, whole and detail below right), now in Berlin, Staatliche Museen, c. 1426.

Facing page, below left: *Adimari Chest* made by Lo Scheggia, detail, in Florence at the Accademia Gallery, c. 1450.

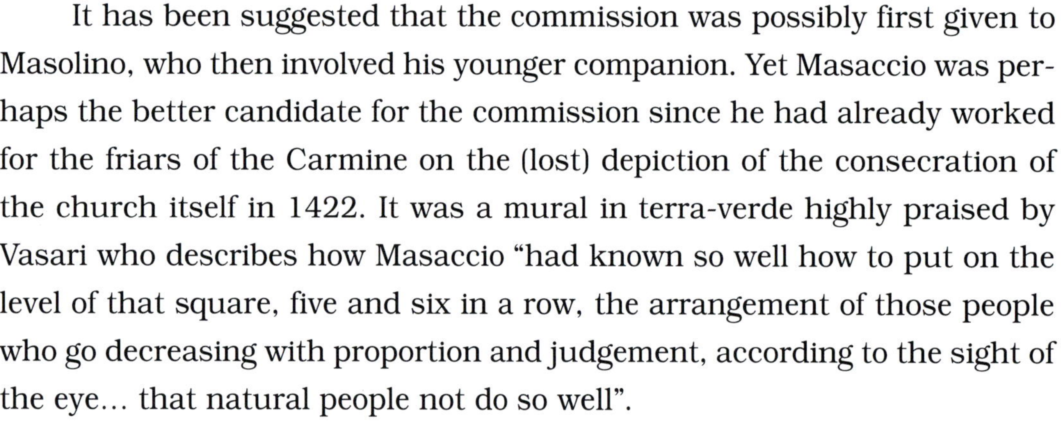

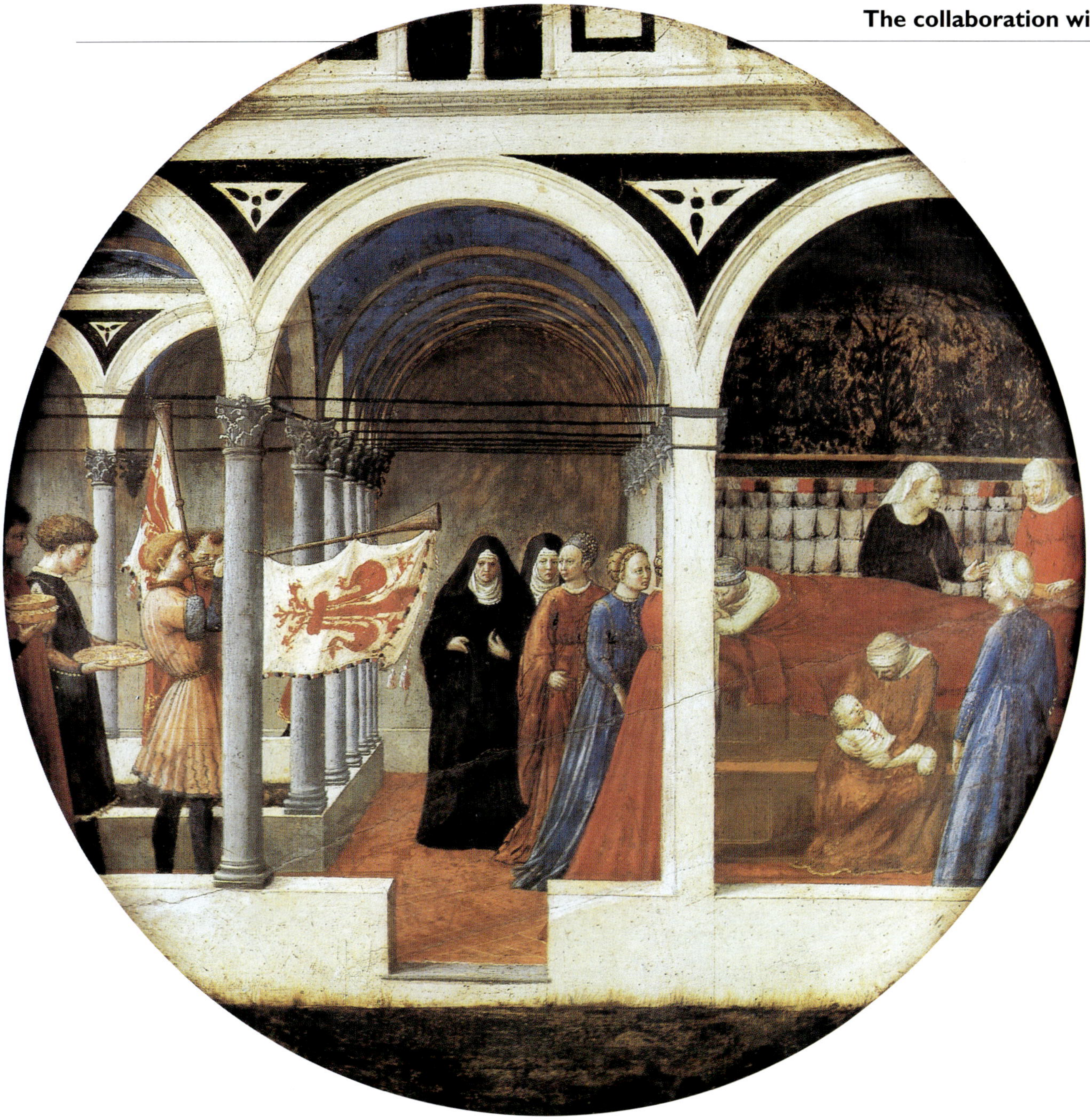

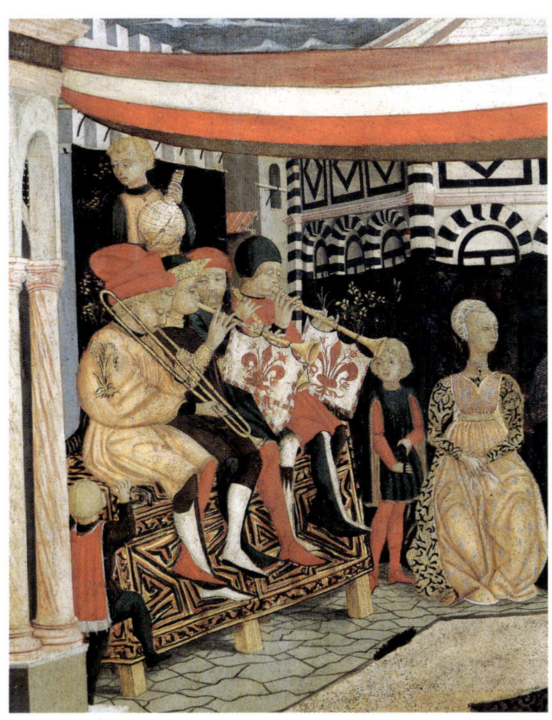

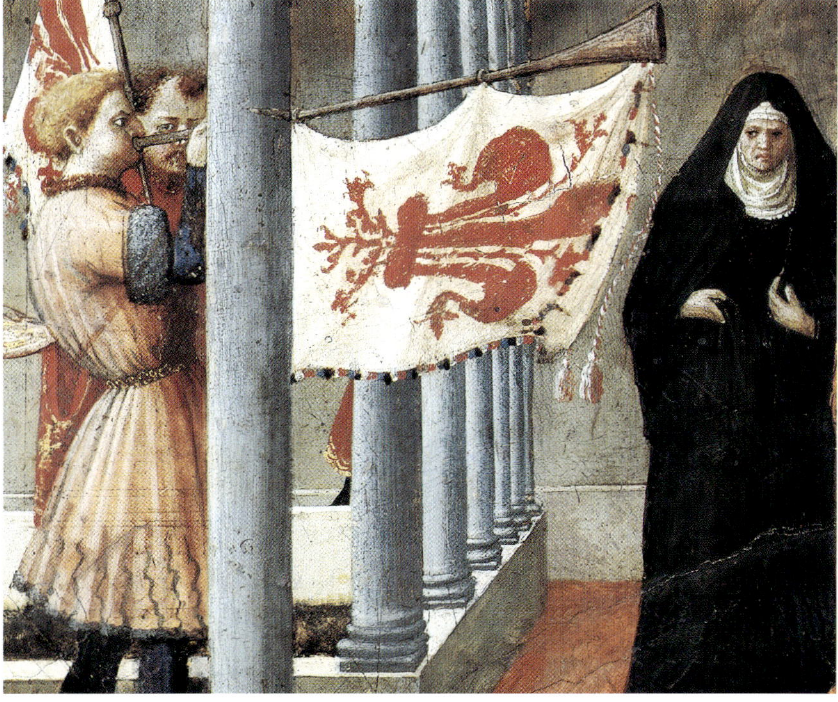

Masolino's documented service in Hungary, Pippo Spano had not recently passed through Florence; indeed, he was absent since 1410. Florentine fiscal documents imply, however, a specific choice of Masolino on his part: "Messer Filippo Scolari has removed him from Florence and had him taken to Hungary, to perform some exercise at the ministry appertaining to the said master Tommaso".

A statement that has lead many to presuppose direct knowledge (or by reputation) of Masolino on the part of the Florentine noble prior to 1425, i.e. that Masolino could have left Florence in the retinue of Pippo Spano already in 1410. A fact that would explain the silence of the Florentine documents on the artist before 1422 and the ease and rapidity with which Masolino abandoned Florence and such an on-going activity as the "compagnia" with Masaccio and the work on the Brancacci to take off for a distant land made dangerous by continual incursions by the Turks, as a result of one of which Pippo Spano was to die shortly afterwards.

Masolino's departure for Hungary, apart perhaps from offering Masaccio the chance to finish the Brancacci commission by himself, left him on his own for about two years. An effort is usually made to date to this period the creation of some works of dubious authorship such as the *Madonna of Humility*, in the National Gallery of Washington, and the *Birthing-stool*, now in Berlin. The first could be the "colmo" (a painting, that is, destined to private devotion or in any case minor, shaped like a tabernacle, with pointed cusps and small side pillars, in the technical language of the time) spoken of in a document of 1426, when Masaccio is sued in the Tribunale di Mercatanzia by a certain Tommaso di Jacopo, squirrel-fur merchant, for a debt of three gold florins and eight lire "discounted the price and the value of an Our Lady in an existing tabernacle, for the said Tommaso squirrel-fur merchant had from the said Tommaso painter". The size of the Washington painting and the shape of the support are such as to warrant the description of "colmo" but, even taking into account the very poor state of the work as a result of the abysmal restorations it has undergone in the course of its long history on the antiques market, the technical characteristics of the painting are very different from those of Masaccio and urge one, instead, towards a date some decades later, in the direction of Domenico Veneziano.

As for the delightful *Birthing-stool* (the back of which is undoubtedly close to Lo Scheggia), the complex but incongruous and misunderstood perspective construction of the buildings induce one to consider it a derivation from Masaccio, the work of some member of the workshop who perhaps worked on his perspective notes without fully understanding

The felicitous and graceful figure of the child in the *Pisa Polyptych*, eating grapes and licking his fingers, transmutes into an image of domestic naturalness the theologically significant motif of the Eucharistic sacrifice. It is the Mother, the Virgin, central in Carmelite spirituality, who in handing him the grapes offers him the sacrifice, thus interceding for the salvation of mankind.

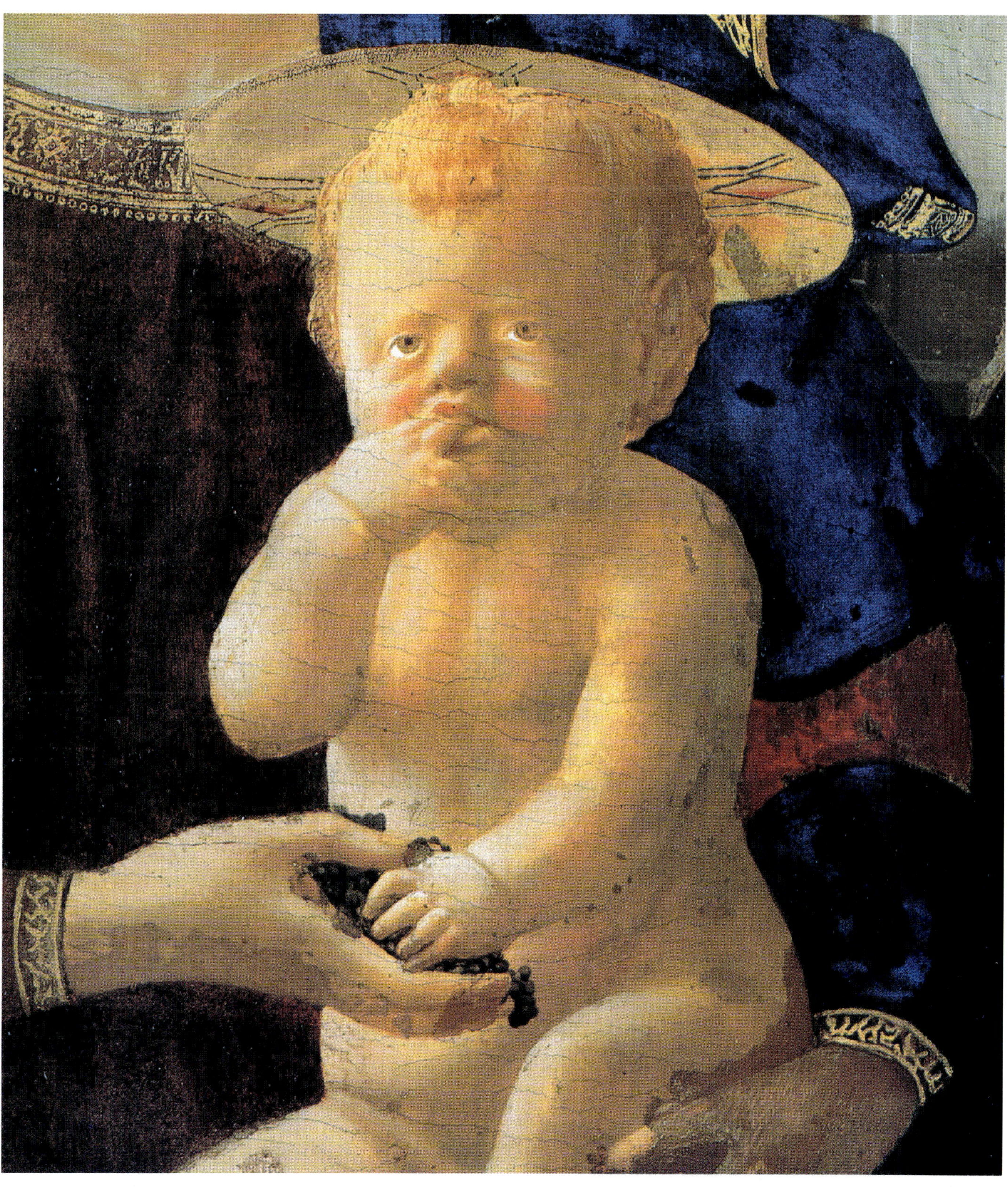

them, as in the case of the *Liberation of the possessed man* in the Philadelphia Museum of Art. Again to 1426 belongs the only work dated by Masaccio and attributed to him by documentation, the now dismembered polyptych for a chapel in the chancel of the church of Santa Maria del Carmine
in Pisa, for the complex tale of which, historical and material, reference
should be made to the specific description (pp. 56-61).

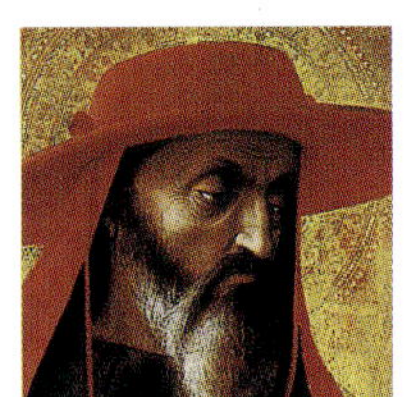

In Rome

According to the agreement Masolino was to stay three years with Filippo Scolari in Hungary, beginning from 1 September 1425, but because of his patron's death his stay concluded earlier. According to the Florentine documents the artist was considered freed from his contract from the end of December 1426, in coincidence with the death of Scolari. There is no trace of the presence of Masolino in Florence, however, for a long time after. In the July of the following year, in the "portata" to the land registry, his father says of him: "he is in Hungary". In parallel the story of Masaccio, in this last slice of his life, seems in some way like that of the elder partner. While Masolino was in Hungary, Masaccio, as we have seen, continued to work in autonomous fashion, in Pisa as well as Florence. In late 1426 or at the beginning of 1427 he must have created the little gem of the *Madonna and Child* (known as *Madonna del Solletico*, "Tickling Madonna"), produced as an object for private devotion for Antonio Casini, made cardinal by Pope Martin V in 1426. The work can be dated with a certain exactitude since it carries on the back Casini's coat-of-arms surmounted by the cardinal's hat.

In July 1427 Masaccio wrote in his own hand and delivered in person his land registry "portata". From then on, however, nothing more is known until, presumably in June 1428, another hand wrote an addition in the margin of the land registry to the effect: "it is said he died in Rome". It would thus seem that both Masolino and Masaccio were away from Florence at the same time for about a year. Certainly, all the sources agree, they were in Rome, where Masaccio was to die shortly afterwards. It would thus seem plausible that, when Pippo Spano died, Masolino went directly to Rome from Hungary; the commissions obtained there would have urged him to seek out his old partner and persuade him to join him in the city of the popes. The contacts made by Masolino in Rome seem to have been of great importance already in the initial phase of his stay. Together with

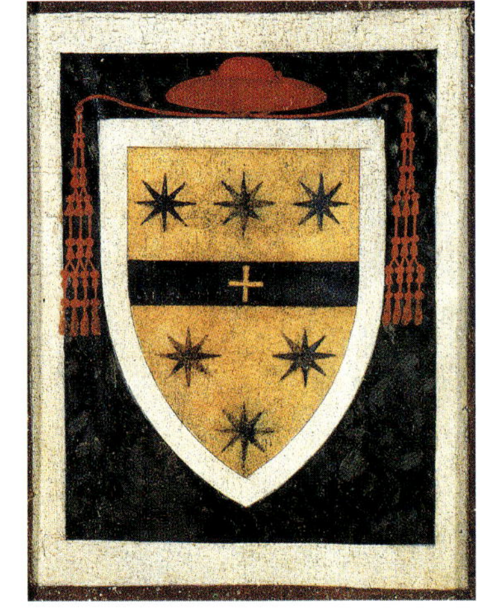

Madonna and Child, front and back with the arms of Cardinal Casini, c. 1426-1427. Florence, Uffizi Gallery.

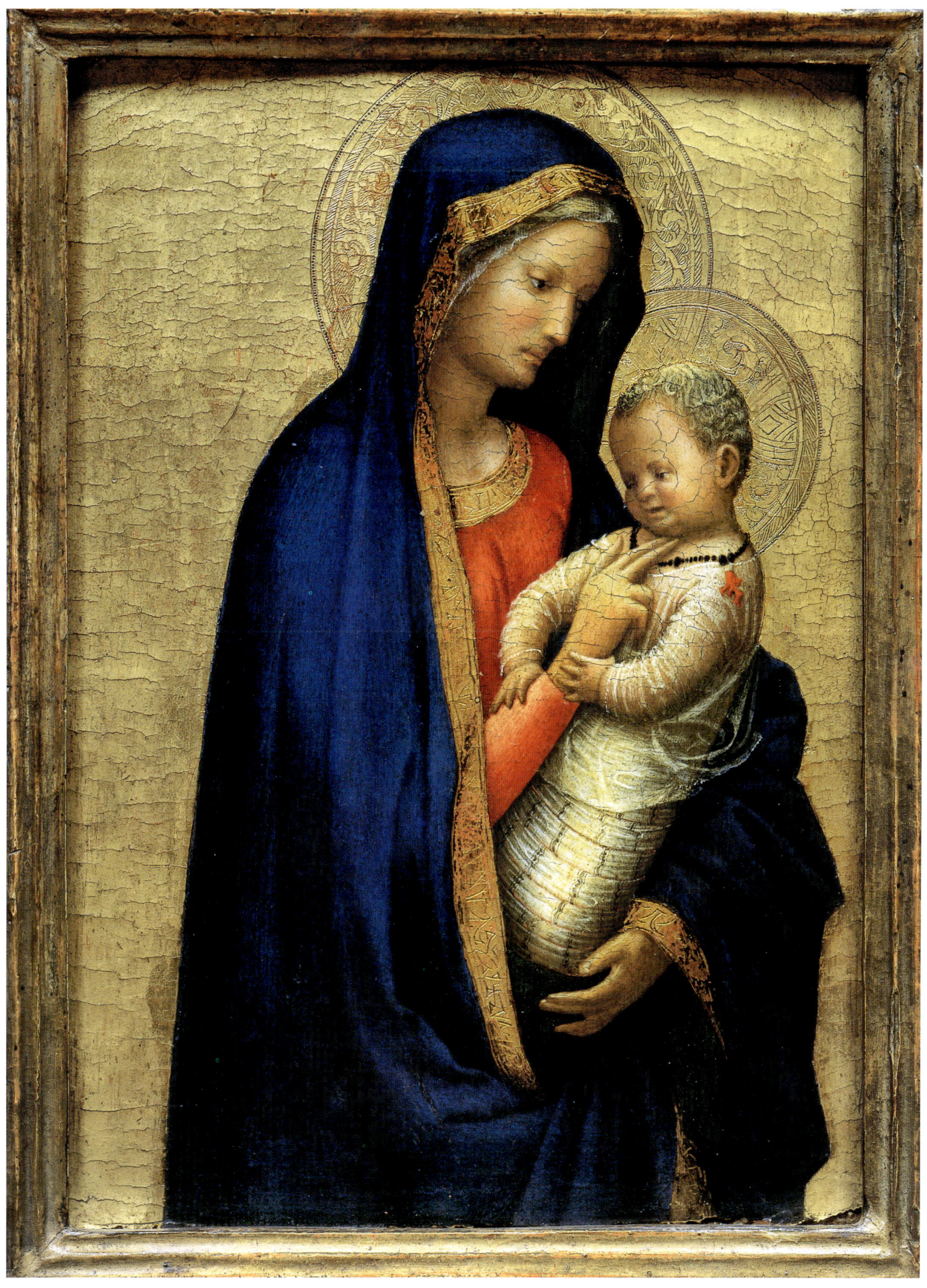

Masaccio he took on the creation of a double-faced polyptych commissioned by the Colonnas (perhaps even by Pope Martin V himself, born Oddone Colonna) for the basilica of Santa Maria Maggiore. The iconography of the polyptych was conceived in close relation to its setting. The main section narrates the miracle of the August snowfall on the Esquiline hill which indicated to Pope Liborius the site and the precise outline on which to build the basilica. On the corresponding main panel is shown the assumption of the Virgin between choirs of angels: the feast of the Assumption was celebrated in Santa Maria Maggiore with a great procession during which the miraculous image of Christ was carried from the Sancta Sanctorum to the Marian basilica. The choice of the saints in the side panels of the polyptych refer to devotions proper to the basilica, which held relics of St Jerome and the Apostle Mathias. Furthermore the conversion and baptism of the man who was then to become Pope Liborius, the founder of the basilica, was attributed to St Jerome. St Martin Bishop was doubtless chosen in honour of the reigning pope, Martin V. In all probability it is a portrait of the pope himself, but undeniably the badge of his family, the column, which appears on the embroidered hem of his chasuble, is a very clear honorific reference to the man. Peter and Paul are *ad evidentiam* Roman saints, patron-saints of the Church; along with St John the Evangelist, the fourth saint portrayed in the polyptych, are the titulars of the other three great basilicas in Rome (Saint Peter's in the Vatican, San Paolo fuori le Mura and San Giovanni in Laterano). St John the Baptist could be a reference to the Florentine provenance of the artists themselves, as well as an homage to the city in which Martin V had found refuge and backing during the first troubled period of his pontificate. St Gregory is, along with St Jerome, one of the Fathers of the Eastern Church and, among them, the only to rise to the papal throne, a particularly important element in a polyptych of papal commissioning.

We do not know which other elements (predellas, pinnacles, pilasters) completed the polyptych, which must have been complex and rich, however, since it was destined to the high altar of the basilica, as seems certain from its being painted on both sides. Vasari, who mentions it with a certain deference, in that it had earned special appreciation from the "divine" Michelangelo, saw it when it had already been moved from its original position to a minor altar of the Colonnas, and does not even mention its being double-faced (was it perhaps no longer visible from both sides?). At some unknown date, probably in the seventeenth century, the polyptych was dismembered, the faces sawn apart along their thickness to obtain separate panels and after passing through the hands of various collectors,

Miracle of the Snow and *Our Lady of the Assumption*, done by Masolino for the *Colonna Polyptych* and now in the Capodimonte Museum in Naples, 1427-1428.

We do not know which of the two central faces of the polyptych for Santa Maria Maggiore in Rome faced the congregation and which was reserved to the more restricted veneration of the canons. Undoubtedly the Virgin surrounded by choirs of angels, rich in precious material, lacquers and metal leaf, lent herself well to public veneration by her magniloquent splendour. Perhaps the, narrative scene was instead destined to the canons, not least because only from close-to would it have been possible to appreciate the numerous characters realistically portrayed on it.

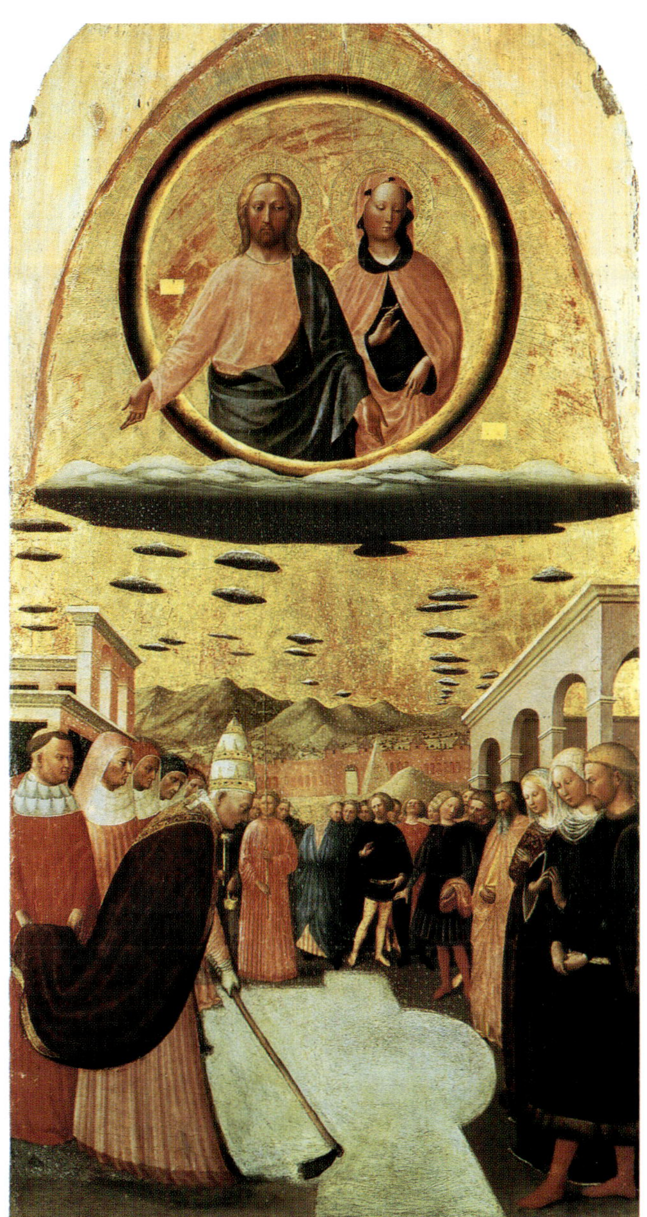
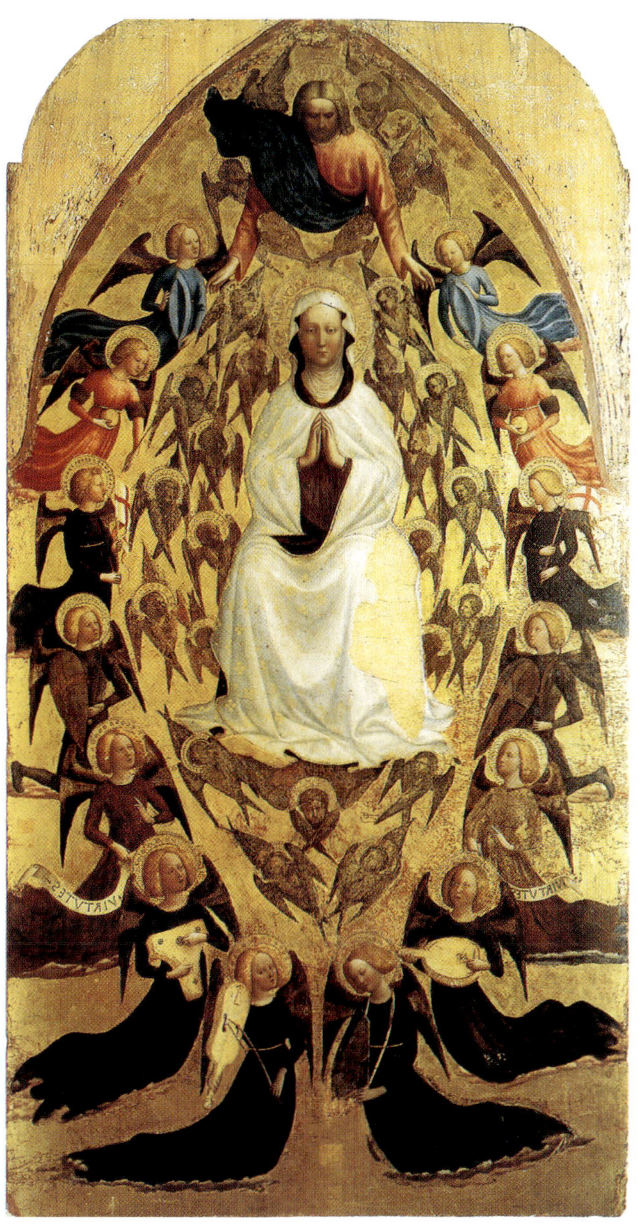

the two central faces (*Miracle of the Snow* and *Our Lady of the Assumption*) passed from the Farnese collection to the Capodimonte Museum in Naples; two of the side panels (*St Jerome and St John the Baptist*; *St Gregory and St Mathias*) to the National Gallery in London; the other two (*St John the Evangelist and St Martin*; *St Peter and St Paul*) to the Philadelphia Museum of Art. All these panels were painted by Masolino except for the one with St Jerome and St John the Baptist, which is by Masaccio, plausibly his last work before his sudden death in Rome. We do not know at what point during the work this dramatic break occurred, nor whether the apparent preponderance of Masolino is only a result of his having to deal with the remaining task on his own.

The general design of the work must have been dealt with at the beginning, for the whole complex at the same time, since it required aspects of an iconographic sort and "hypertextual" links between the various sections.

For example the gestures of the saints in the side panels, the play of gazes, were designed so as to have meaning in relation to the central sections. So too the slope of the ground on which the saints stand (upwards in the sections with St Peter and St Paul, and St Gregory and St Mathias, downwards in the sections with St Jerome and St John the Baptist, and St John the Evangelist and St Martin) is no accident, guided as it is by lines cut during preparation. Perhaps, since it is an element common to the pairs of linked saints, it can serve as an indication of an iconological kind for matching them in correspondence with the central scene: the ground slopes up from earth to heaven in the presence of the Assumption, whereas it slopes down to the terrestrial scene of the miracle of summer snow on the Esquiline.

Just as important were the technical element, of the sequence of the various stages, that required a planned scheme for the work. Each panel had be dressed, gessoed on both sides, but more important the gilding had to be done in a single stage and that meant that all six scenes had to be planned in advance, given that the gilder worked according to lines to separate the spaces to be gilded from those to be painted: lines provided by the painter. Once one has taken account of these stages and thanks to the help of scientific investigation techniques one can work out the progress of the work. We know in fact that the Philadelphia panels (*St Peter and St Paul* and *St John the Evangelist and St Martin*) underwent changes. It was not simply a matter of an inversion of position of the saints within the two pairs. In the panels with St Peter and St Paul the initial stage of painting had been done by Masaccio.

Since he had left it incomplete, presumably because of his sudden death, Masolino had to take over, among other things partly covering some of the already completed work so as to bring it closer to his own style. It is possible therefore to suggest that Masaccio had reserved for himself the side panels with the figures of saints, plausible also because of his interest in the great sculptural figures derived from Donatello. Presumably the two artists worked side by side: while Masaccio was arranging the side panels, Masolino was preparing the central scenes.

It remains, however, interesting to grasp the reasons for the change of position of the saints in the Philadelphia panels. It is highly likely that for the one with St John and St Martin the decision was taken so as to emphasise the figure of the latter, setting it in profile rather than frontally: the features of the portrait would thus be recognisable. The change of position between St Peter and St Paul seems instead to be linked to Roman iconographical traditions: in the mosaic in the apse of Santa Maria Maggiore, as in apse mosaics in other churches (including the lost one in the old Saint

St Jerome and St John the Baptist, whole and details, 1427-1428. London, National Gallery.

The two saints, the last work of Masaccio's brief life, reveal a profound research in the anatomical rendering and the volumetrics of the bodies, study of light and interest in description. There is another highly successful example of an animal (Masaccio could have seen lions in Florence, given that they were kept in special pens, in Palazzo Vecchio, as "totem" symbols of the city); the detail of the crumpled pages of the book; the little model of a church held by St Jerome which is a small perspectively defined building, complete with sculptural element on the facade; the naturalistic flowery meadow, with recognisable botanical species.

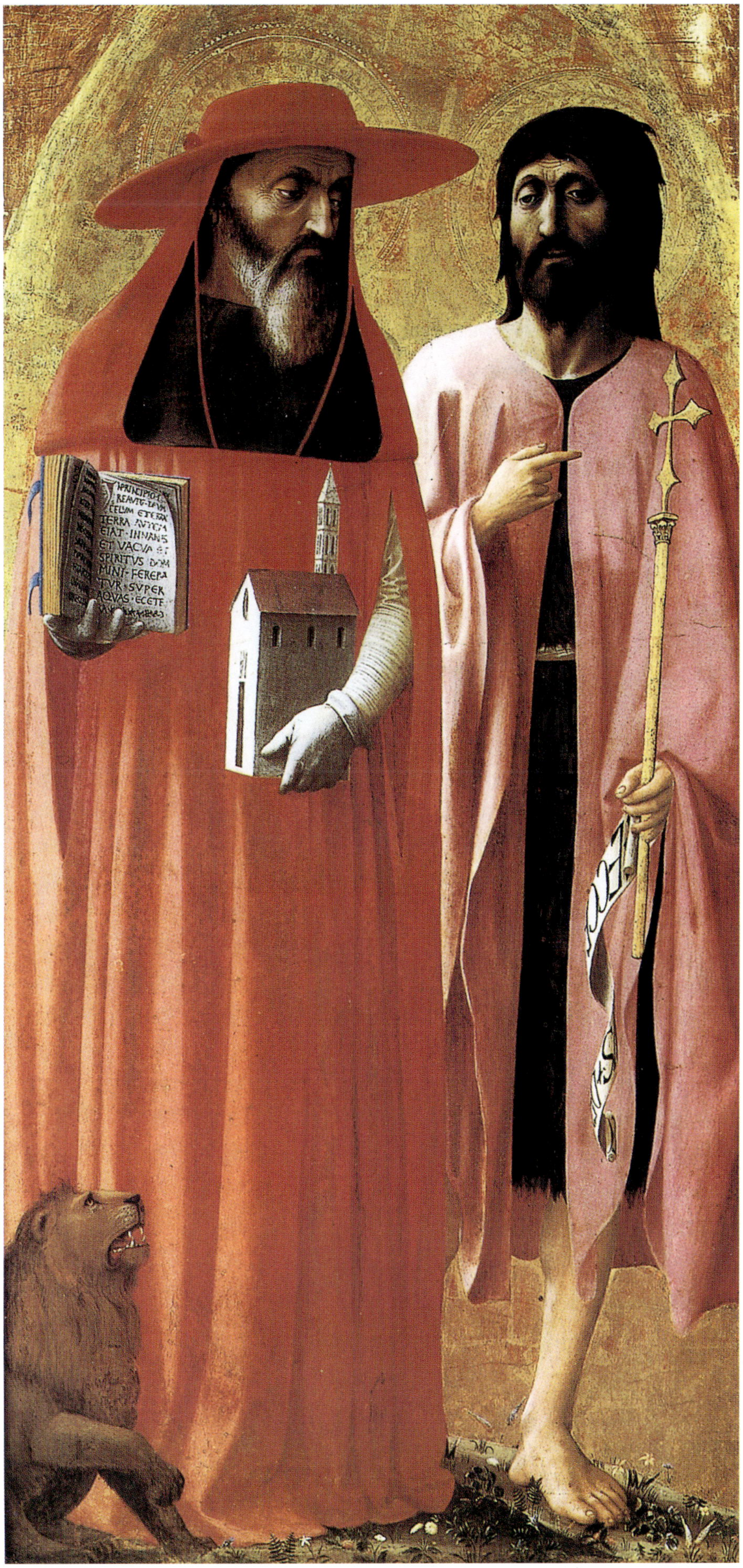

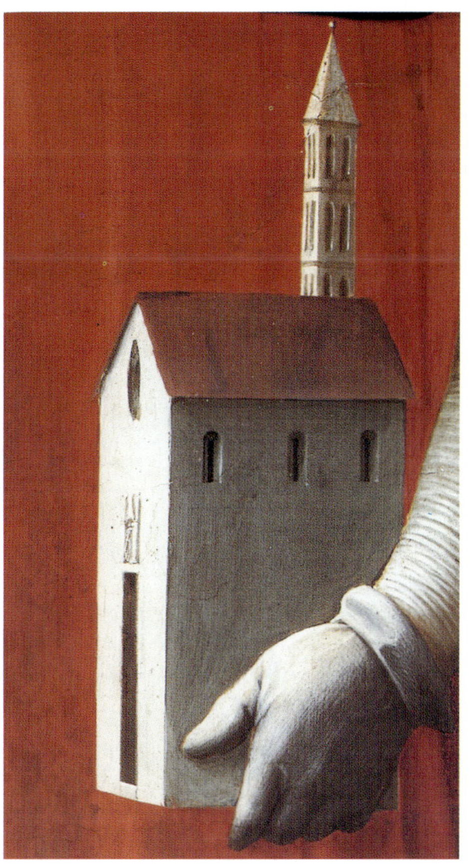

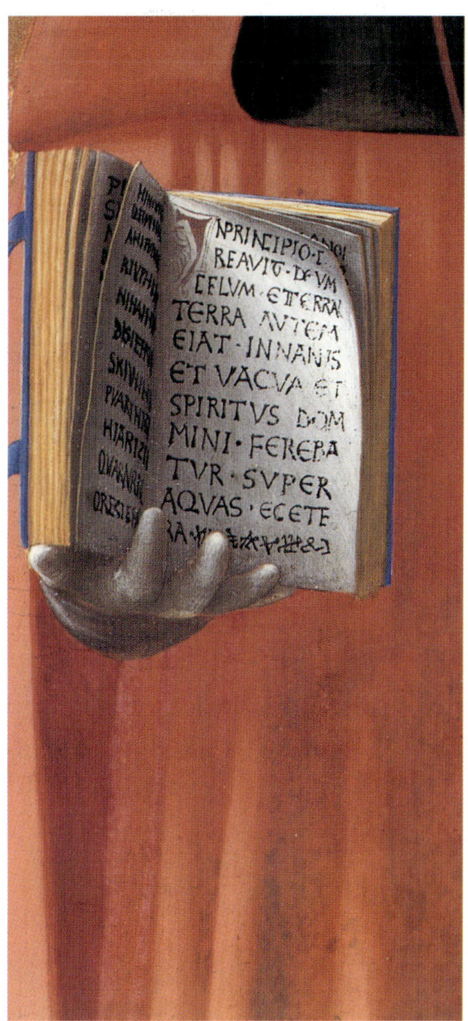

Peter's), the two saints appear in that position, Peter on the right and Paul on the left. The initial mistake in their positioning was probably connected with the Florentine artists' ignorance of the tradition.

Masolino, at this point only due to the death of Masaccio, return to Florence, in May 1428. It was then he finally became independent of his father: an act postponed for long years so as to have someone to administer his affairs and finances at home and which, precisely because of this tardy resolution, seems to indicate the painter's need to act elsewhere on his own behalf, as well as being a sharp break with Florence. He was to come back only a year later, in March 1429, to pick up the notable sum of 300 florins, and then never again. The close relation with Masaccio was to be unforgettable for Masolino, who for the rest of his career strove to infuse volumetrics, naturalism and perspective into his modernized late Gothic vision. Out from under the yoke of the strongly charismatic personality of his young co-worker he finally returned in the fancifully "perspective" buildings of his Rome and Castiglione Olona to frescoes whose story-telling guise was certainly more congenial to him, with a dash of decorativism that was well suited to the telling of medieval fables.

Masolino's sudden return to Florence in May 1428 would thus seem have been motivated by the need to procure money and legal status at the death of Masaccio. And who, if not Masolino, could have brought the news of the death of his young partner which was reported as a certainty by the land register officials in that year of 1428? The formula in which they register the death, "dicesi", it's said, is not in fact the report of hearsay, but a legal formula of trustworthiness, equivalent to "it is testified".

The short year of Masaccio spent in Rome (no more than ten months, taking into consideration the whole period between the "portata" to the land registry and the registration of his death, but very likely somewhat less) gave ample time for starting on the creation of the polyptych for Santa Maria Maggiore: contacts with those who had commissioned it and working out the subject-matter with them; for finding places and skilled labour *in situ*; for getting in touch with the commercial and legal milieu dealing with art work in Rome; for planning the work while the wooden structure was being put together; for the preparatory stages of layers, drawing, gilding, with all the precautions and the double waiting-times between one stage and the next made necessary by the double-faced support. And finally the actual completion by Masaccio of one section and groundwork done for at least one of the other. Before the suspension of work caused by the sudden death that was to make Brunelleschi exclaim: "We have suffered a most grievous loss in Masaccio".

St Jerome and St John the Baptist, detail, 1427-1428. London, National Gallery.

The psychological intensity that Masaccio conferred on his characters derived undoubtedly from the rethinking of classical creations begun in statuary. The attitudes and the expressions diffused the new humanist conception of the individual and the virtues of dignity and self-awareness that it endorsed.

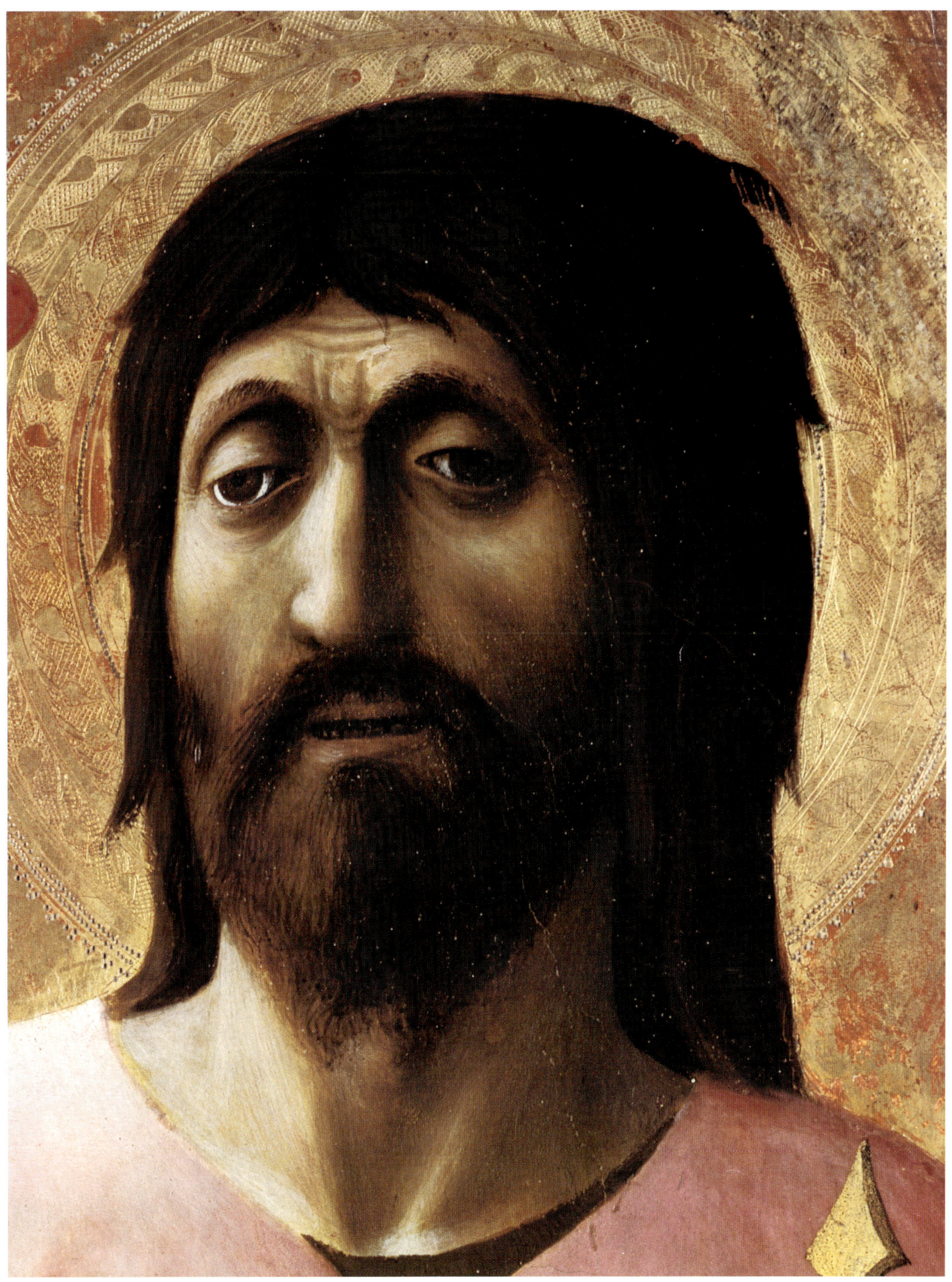

Chronology	1401	1412	1417	1418	1421
Masaccio	Tommaso is born in Castel San Giovanni (the present San Giovanni Valdarno) to the notary Ser Giovanni di Mone d'Andreuccio and Jacopa di Martinozzo di Dino. According to the late declaration of his younger brother, Giovanni known as Lo Scheggia, he was born on 21 December.	Their mother, widowed in 1406, remarries the druggist Tedesco di Maestro Feo; Masaccio probably does not go with his mother to his stepfather's house, but stays with his father's family.	Sometime in this year he moves to Florence, to the Parish of San Niccolò Oltrarno.	In October Tommaso, who is described as "dipintore", acts as guarantor for an artisan of San Giovanni Valdarno who joins the Arte dei Legnaiuoli, evidence of a certain financial and social standing.	Mariotto di Cristofano marries Caterina, Masaccio's stepsister. Lo Scheggia is shown by the documents to be in the workshop of Bicci di Lorenzo along with Andrea di Giusto Manzini, but there is no evidence to suggest the presence of Masaccio.
Florence	**1401** The Arte di Calimala announces the competition for the second door of the Baptistery: Ghiberti wins the commission beating Brunelleschi, whose mould with the *Sacrifice of Isaac* becomes the manifesto of the new trends. **1407** Funerary monument to Ilaria del Carretto by Jacopo della Quercia.	The major Florentine sculptors, including Ghiberti, Donatello and Nanni di Banco, are engaged on the decoration of the cathedral, Giotto's Campanile and the church of Orsanmichele.	Donatello finishes the *St George* for the Arte dei Corazzai in Orsanmichele with the altarpiece, the first artistic application of Brunelleschi's theories. Lorenzo Monaco enrolls among the Florentine painters.	**1418** Brunelleschi wins the competition for the dome of the cathedral, financed by the Arte di Calimala: he is master-mason together with Ghiberti. Two years later work begins on the dome, which is completed in 1436. **1419** Work begins on the Spedale degli Innocenti to Brunelleschi's design.	The first works of Fra Angelico date to the early '20s. In 1420 Brunelleschi makes the *Crucifix* for the Gondi chapel in Santa Maria Novella, in competition, according to tradition, with that by Donatello in Santa Croce. The following year Filippo Lippi takes vows in the Carmine monastery.
Rome	**1402-1404** First visits to Rome of Donatello and Brunelleschi to study antique art. **1410** Alexander V begins the work of enlarging the Vatican palaces.	**1416** Lorenzo and Jacopo Salimbeni fresco the oratory of San Giovanni in Urbino with the *Stories of John the Baptist* and a *Crucifixion*.	Oddone Colonna becomes Pope as Martin V. In 1419 he meets Gentile da Fabriano in Brescia and invites him to Rome in view of the plan for artistic renewal of the city.	**1420** Martin V makes his entry into Rome after the long absence of the papacy: the city is bleak and the pope sets up a magistracy for the planning of urban and architectural interventions. Piero della Francesca is born in Città di Castello.	The renewal of the city goes on: the cardinals also back the restoration of churches, basilicas and palaces to recreate the image of Rome as a centre of power.
Milan and Bologna	The *Notebook of drawings* by Giovannino de' Grassi, architect of the cathedral dates to the start of the century. In 1401 he is succeeded as director of the site by Michelino da Besozzo, painter and master-glassmaker.	Michelino da Besozzo paints the *Adoration of the Magi* in the Avignon Book of Hours. In Bologna Giovanni da Modena goes on with the frescoes in San Petronio (Bolognini Chapel).	Gentile da Fabriano is paid for an altar table destined to Carlo Malatesta, Lord of Rimini.	**1418** The high altar of Milan cathedral is consecrated. Gentile is in the service of Pandolfo Malatesta in Brescia. **1420** Michelino da Besozzo paints the *Mystic Marriage of St Catherine*. Frescoes by Giovanni da Modena in the chapel of Sts Abbondius and George in San Petronio.	The statue of *Martin V* for Milan cathedral dates from this year, sole documented work of Jacopino da Tradate, active in the Fabbrica till 1425.
Venice	**1408** Gentile da Fabriano comes from Central Italy to work on the Ducal Palace. Around 1410 Michelino da Besozzo also stays in Verona and Venice. Sometime in these years Domenico Veneziano is born.	**1415** Pisanello and Gentile work together on the decoration of the Sala del Maggior Consiglio in the Ducal Palace with *Stories of Barbarossa*. Between 1410 and 1420 Jacobello del Fiore produces the polyptych with *Stories of St Lucy*.	Gentile, appreciated in many courts between Padua, Verona and Brescia, from 1414 leaves Venice for Fabriano.	**1418-1419** To the end of the second decade can be dated the *Madonna of the rose garden* by Stefano da Verona, influenced by northern court Gothic. **1420** Pisanello paints one of his first works, the *Madonna of the quail*.	The brothers Bartolomeo and Giovanni Bon, along with Matteo Ravetti, design the Ca' d'Oro for Doge Contarini, a masterpiece of late Gothic architecture.

1422 — 7 January he enrolls in the Arte dei Medici e Speziali: described as "pictor" of the Parish of San Niccolò Oltrarno. The date 23 April is inscribed on the triptych found in the little church of San Giovenale near Reggello. In October he pays two liras to the chamberlain of the guild.

1424 — This year he joins, along with Masolino, the Compagnia di San Luca, the association of Florentine painters: what probably drove the two artists to regularise their position was some important commission, for example the *St Anne Metterza* for Sant'Ambrogio.

1425 — Together with an older painter, Niccolò di ser Lapo, he has a workshop in Sant'Apollinare: the two are paid for gilding procession candlesticks by the Bishop of Fiesole. In July he appears as debtor to the grocer Bartolomeo di Lorenzo.

1426 — Payments relating to the *Pisa Polyptych* follow one another from February to December, sometimes in the painter's absence. In April he pays taxes in San Giovanni Valdarno along with his brother. In August he is found among the debtors of the fur trader Tommaso di Jacopo, to whom he offers a *Madonna* in partial payment of the debt.

1427 — In January his presence in Pisa is again documented. In July he presents the land registry "portata" with his brother : they live in rented quarters and with their mother in via de' Servi. He has a workshop near the Badia Fiorentina.

1428 — After 20 June there is news of his death in Rome. the *Libro di Antonio Billi*, which reports Brunelleschi's famous comment, offers the unlikely suggestion that he was poisoned; other sources (Cristoforo Landino and Antonio Manetti) give 1427 as the year of his death.

1422 Masolino in Florence. Brunelleschi designs the Sagrestia Vecchia for the Basilica di San Lorenzo, restructured in 1419. **1423** *Adoration of the Magi* by Gentile da Fabriano for the Strozzi chapel in Santa Trinita. Masolino paints the *Madonna* now in Bremen.

Masolino finishes the frescoes of the Compagnia della Croce in Santo Stefano degli Agostiniani in Empoli. In Siena Sassetta paints the *Pala dell'Arte della Lana*.

Gentile da Fabriano paints the *Quaratesi Polyptych*, in line with the new Florentine techniques; in May he leaves the city. Ghiberti is employed for the Porta del Paradiso of the Baptistery. In September Masolino leaves for Hungary, called by Pippo Spano. Alesso Baldovinetti is born.

Because of opposition from the nobles the proposed establishing of a Land Registry does not go through. Masaccio works on the polyptych for the Carmine in Pisa, a city where Donatello and Michelozzo are also documented as present.

The Catasto is finally set up. Donatello and Michelozzo, who had opened a workshop in 1425, create the tomb for the anti-pope John XXIII in the Baptistery of Florence. In this same year Donatello begins the *Habakkuk* for the Campanile of the cathedral.

Brunelleschi finishes the Sagrestia Vecchia in San Lorenzo and is engaged for the project for the Santo Spirito. Ghiberti begins work on the third door of the Baptistery, which is finished in 1452.

1422 Arcangelo di Cola, a follower of Gentile, is in the city in the Pope's service probably engaged on the making of votive images for pilgrims. **1423** Martin V proclaims the jubilee.

Martin V carries on with his project to rebuild the city. In the coming years artists such as Gentile, Masolino and Masaccio, Pisanello and Domenico Veneziano will be summoned.

Cardinal Branda Castiglione, Papal Legate very close to Martin V, is in Rome: he will be the client for Masolino's frescoes decorating his chapel in San Clemente.

Masolino comes to Rome on his return from Hungary. Gentile reaches the city to fresco the cycle, now l3ost, of San Giovanni in Laterano.

On the death of Gentile da Fabriano, Pisanello inherits the workshop. He stays till 1433; in these years Donatello and Brunelleschi are often in Rome. Commissioned by the Colonna family Masaccio and Masolino produce the *Colonna Polyptych* for Santa Maria Maggiore.

Masolino frescos the chapel of Cardinal Branda da Castiglione in San Clemente with *Stories of St Catherine and St Ambrose*.

Pisanello is found in Mantova, at the service of the Gonzaga. The next year he is in Pavia: he paints frescoes, now lost, in the Visconti castle.

Leon Battista Alberti studies in Bologna and Padua; a learned interpreter of classic creations, he was to go through his training in Rome in the '30s.

Jacopo della Quercia begins the cycle of reliefs with stories from Old Testament for the portal of San Petronio in Bologna.

Work on the Charterhouse of Pavia intensifies, decided on by Gian Galeazzo Visconti in 1396 in emulation of the cathedral of Milan.

Vincenzo Foppa, one of the major Lombard fifteenth-century painters, was probably born in Brescia; his masterpiece is the Portinari Chapel in Sant'Eustorgio in Milan, frescoed in 1468.

Around 1430 Cosmè Tura is born, leading figure of the Ferrara school.

Many of Pisanello's graphic works, among them the allegory of *Luxury* (now in the Albertina of Vienna), date from the early '20s.

Stefano da Zevio moves to Verona. Pisanello is also there, working on the painted decoration for the *Funerary monument of Niccolò Brenzoni* in San Fermo, sculpted by the Florentine Nanni di Bartolo.

Paolo Uccello, who was to remain in the city until 1430, executes a lost mosaic for St Mark's Basilica.

After finishing the tomb for the Brenzoni, Pisanello leaves Verona for Rome, where he is called by Gentile for work in San Giovanni in Laterano.

The work on enlarging the Ducal Palace is completed, it now joins St Mark's basilica. It will be completed with the construction of the Porta della Carta (1438-1442), work of the Bon brothers.

In 1428 Gentile Bellini is born, son of Jacopo, in 1430 Carlo Crivelli; in Padua, in 1431, Andrea Mantegna is born: they were to be the leading figures of the Venetian school.

SAN GIOVENALE TRIPTYCH

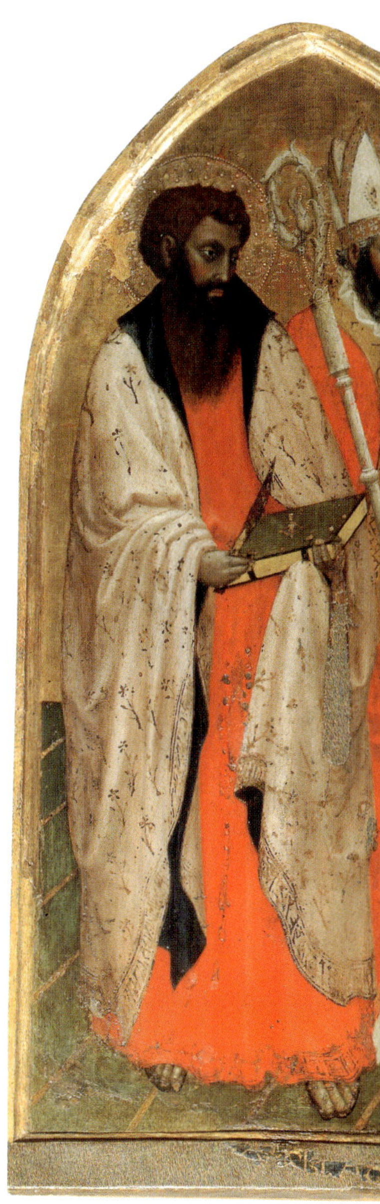

San Giovenale Triptych (Enthroned Madonna and Child with two angels and Sts Bartholomew, Blaise, Giovenale and Anthony the Abbot)
tempera on wood 108 x 65 (central panel), 88 x 44 (side panels); 1422 Cascia di Reggello, church of San Pietro

One of those unhoped-for coincidences that sometimes kiss the brow of art history studies and a passionate concern for one's surroundings: that perhaps is how to look at the finding of the *Triptych* in 1961 in the little church of San Giovenale near Reggello, for which it had been made and where it had remained for 539 years. It was an official working for the Soprintendenza Fiorentina, Luciano Berti, later director of the Uffizi and soprintendente, who recognised Masaccio's work, thereby bringing about its material and cultural restoration. In the course of the centuries the painting had undergone serious structural damage and heavy restoration of the painted surface. As recent investigation has enabled us to make out, the work was not originally a triptych, but an altarpiece with a complex frame, within which the painted area was divided as a triptych: an extremely interesting typology that evinces the evolution of the forms of altarpieces according to the Renaissance style. The painted surface had also been much altered, so much so that even a scholar as learned as Guido Carocci described it in 1890 as coming from the Sienese artistic milieu.

The restoration that followed Berti's felicitous intuition discovered, among other things, gilded lettering in capitals on the lower edge of the *Triptych*. Besides the names of the saints, the inscription records the date of execution: ANNO DOMINI MCCCCXXII A DI VENTITRE D'APRILE. It is therefore the first known work by Masaccio, who at the time was barely twenty-one years old.

Though not mentioned by the sources, the *Triptych* is basic for a reconstruction of Masaccio's work and, despite the undeniable juvenility of some solutions, fundamental also for the painting of the very early Renaissance in its innovative approach to the great perspective and plastic discoveries of Brunelleschi and Donatello: as Vasari says, Masaccio grew up "following as much as he could in the tracks of Filippo and of Donato while art was still different". And in this first stage it seems that Masaccio's enlightenment, his Renaissance epiphany, came above all from Donatello and his statuary. As fresh scientific investigation has brought to light, the volumes of all the figures are sure and the bodies physically take over space. Just like the subjects, the croziers and the books are absolutely sculptural.

From a compositional point of view the space of the *Triptych* is already conceived perspectively. The recession of the lines towards a single central van-

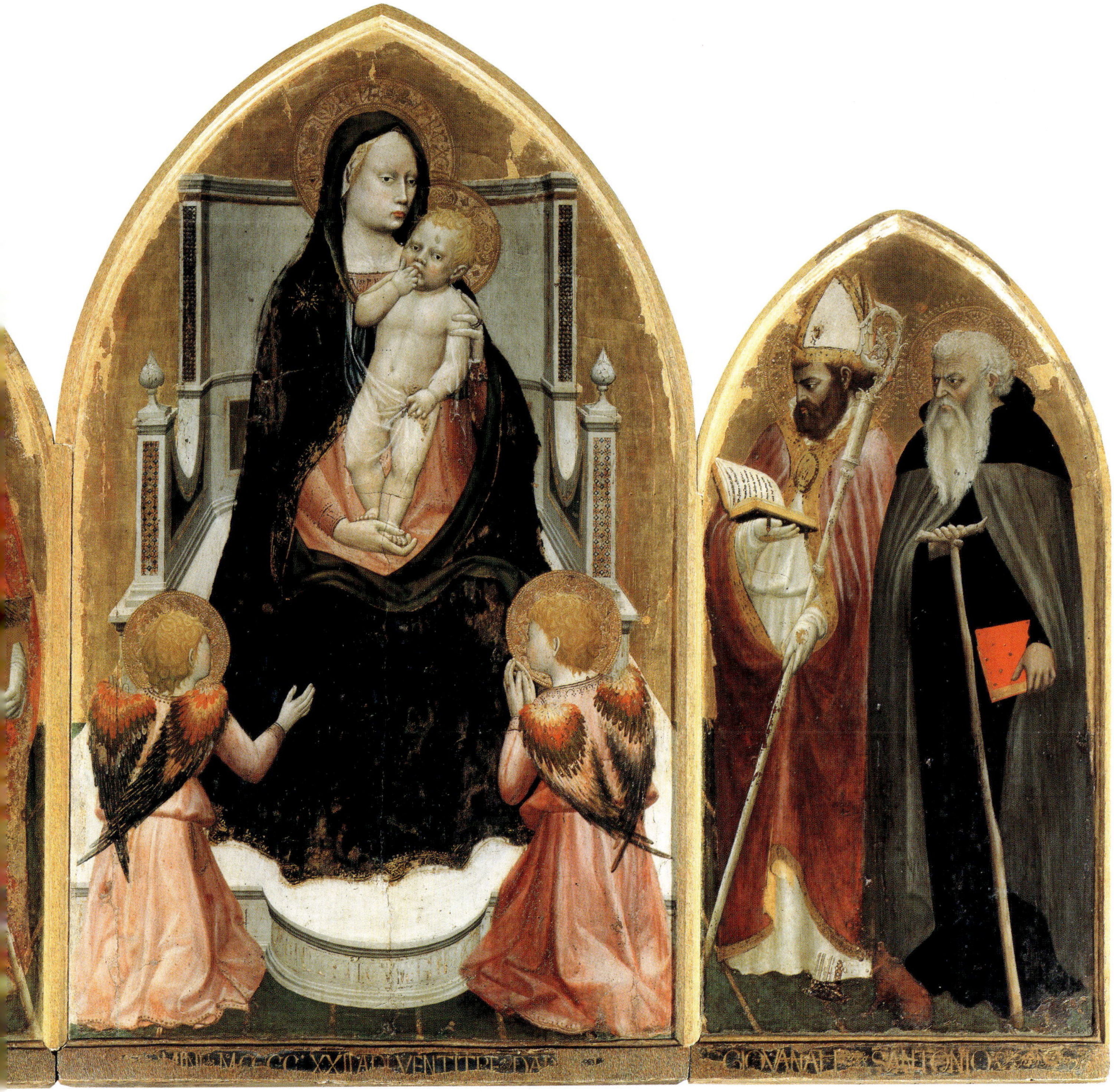

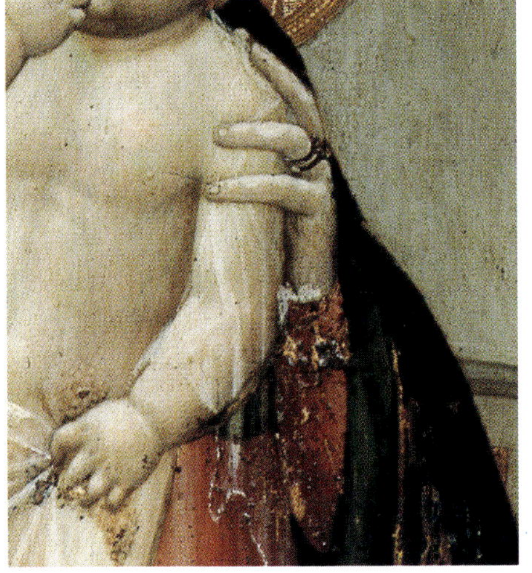

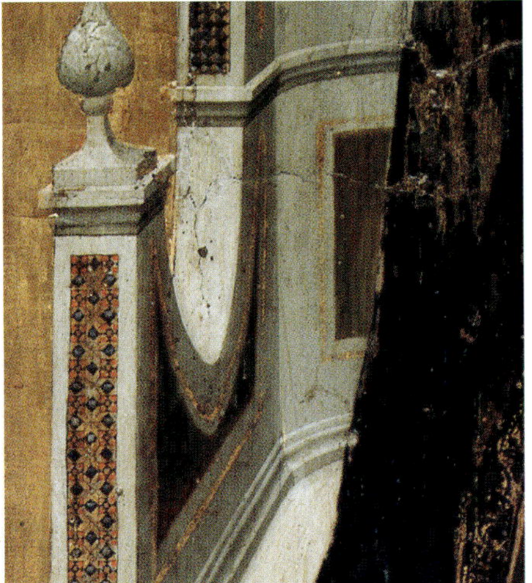

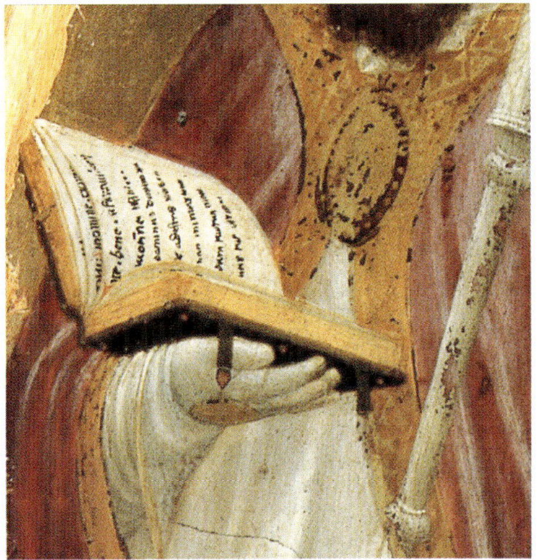

ishing point contributes to giving that effect of tangible reality to the whole composition; the scene in the central section also takes place in real space, the prolungation of that in which the viewer finds himself. The whole disguised by the green floor, often mistaken for a meadow, furrowed by lines of gold converging on the vanishing point. Probably a ruse that reassured a traditional patron such as that of San Giovenale and at the same time gave a wink in the direction of the cultivated viewer: in fact the base unifies the space element in the three sections and the gold lines, possibly, underline it. That knowing viewers went from Florence to admire the work is demonstrated also by the echo in contemporary painting of the architectonic element of the throne of grey stone, enriched by cosmatesque inlays, that in the deep niche-like curvature of the back evokes Giotto and Rome. Besides Donatello and Brunelleschi, in fact, the *Triptych* makes clear the other great source of Masaccio's art, Giotto: his great plastic innovations, his classicality, essentiality and volumetrics were felt by the young artist as a legacy for obligatory going beyond the late Gothic formulae.

Examining the contents of the work in search of indications of the patron and precise detail, the recent interpretation of the date of the inscription, in relation to the book that the eponymous saint is reading, has shed some light. The saint is reciting the antiphon for the first day of the novena for the feast of dedication of the church, which fell on the first day of May. The collocation *in situ* of the painting would thus seem closely linked to the religious life of the Parish of San Giovenale, as the choice of saints portrayed would also lead one to suppose: from St Giovenale himself (a native of Narni and depicted very little elsewhere, his veneration in Cascia seems connected to the history of the translation of his body to Lucca on a road that passed through Valdarno) to Sts Bartholomew, Blaise and Anthony (linked to peasant devotion because of their ability to heal and as protectors of animals and of the attivities connected with farming and stock-breeding, as encapsulated in the marvellous piglet at the feet of St Anthony).

So while in the past the search was for rich patrons and even an original setting in Florence for the *Triptych*, so impossible did it seem that a work of this quality should have such an out-of-the-way destination, now more domestic origins tend to be looked for. That Masaccio should make his debut as an autonomous artist with a work for an area close to his birthplace is very plausible. A guaranty that Masaccio paid around 1420 for a carpenter of Castel San Giovanni is perhaps related to this painting. He might well be the craftsman who made the wooden structure, to whom Masaccio was in some way indebted, to the point later of acting as his guarantor. This might then explain the innovative form of the original *Triptych*: Masaccio would have been directly involved, whereas painters usually were not, in this stage of working. Furthermore, to execute the painting in San Giovanni, in the workshop of his grandfather, would have saved the young painter having to pay the customs for taking out of Florence a work made in city, something about which artists were particularly concerned, to the extent that some had workshops outside the walls of Florence meant for paintings destined to the surrounding countryside.

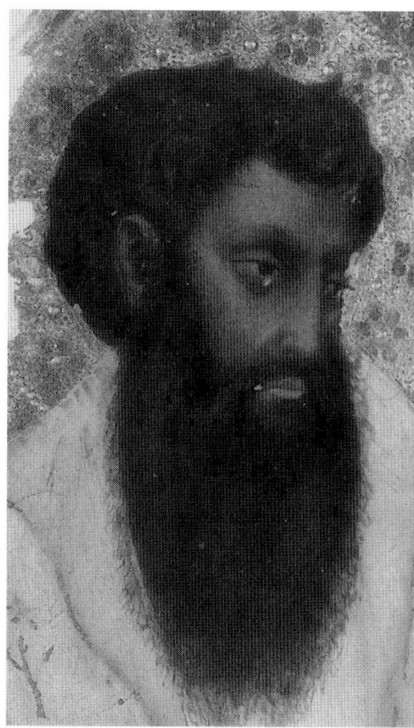

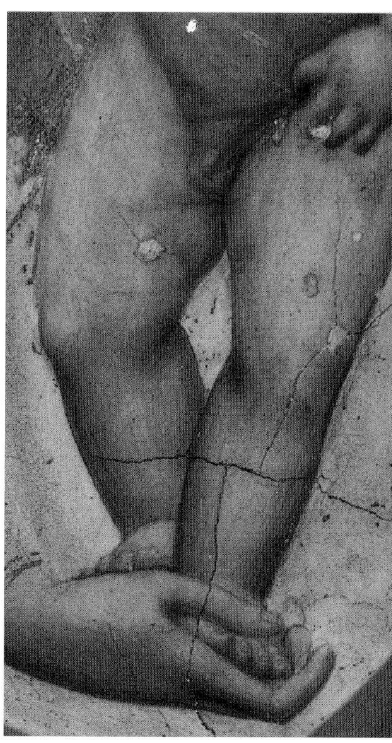

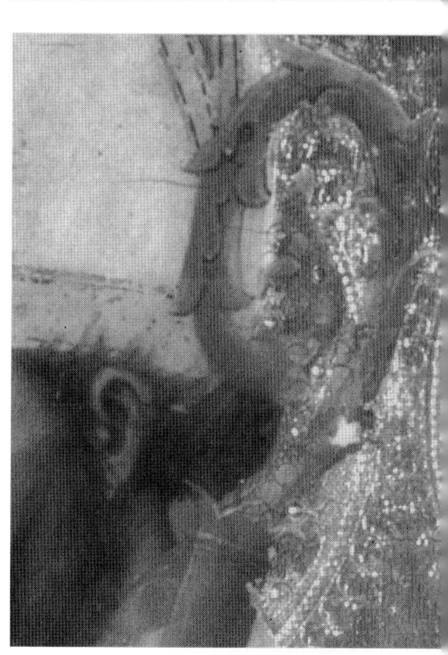

Facing page:
San Giovenale Triptych, infra-red reflectography, detail of St Bartholomew, of the Child and of the crozier of St Giovenale.

Right:
San Giovenale Triptych, detail of the right-hand panel with Sts Giovenale and Anthony the Abbot.

The very recent infra-red reflectography makes it possible to see the preparatory layers of the painting, i.e. the stage in which Masaccio began to draw his composition. What comes out particularly clearly is the naturalistic rendering of limbs and volumes that recalls the contemporary sculpture of Donatello.

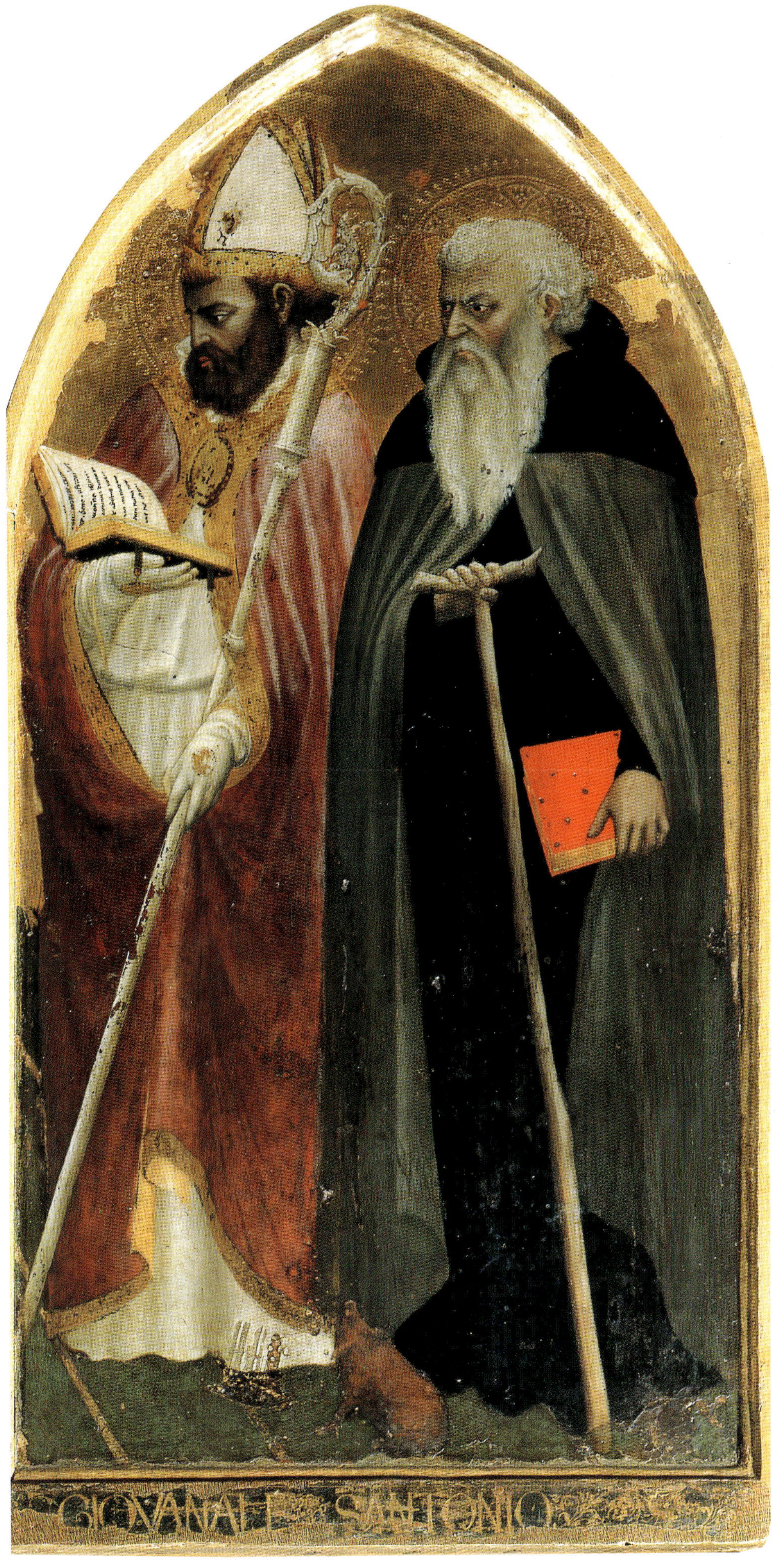

BRANCACCI CHAPEL

View of the Brancacci Chapel, in the right transept of the church of Santa Maria del Carmine in Florence

Facing page:
The expulsion of Adam and Eve from Paradise
fresco
208 x 88;
c. 1424-1426

The decoration of the chapel is the pivotal episode in the relation between Masaccio and Masolino and the determining event for Florentine artistic culture in the early fifteenth century. From the mid-fourteenth century the Brancacci, merchants who made their fortune in the silk trade, possessed a chapel in Santa Maria del Carmine, to decorate which they several times left bequests. In the third decade of the fifteenth century the interests of Felice Brancacci, an emergent politician very successful, focused again on the chapel. It was probably after his diplomatic mission to Cairo on behalf of the Florentine republic, from which he returned in February 1423, that the idea came to realisation. No certain documents exist on the matter, so much so that the real involvement of the Brancacci family in the choosing of iconography and of artists is debatable, and the alternative proposal is for direct supervision by the Carmelites. The interpretation of the Stories of St Peter, a rare subject in Florence, as exaltation of the political figure of Felice Brancacci – rich from sea trading and several times governor of Pisa and Livorno – and of his role in the public finances of Florence is now less immediate because of the loss of scenes, in the vault and large lunettes, of *The boat* and

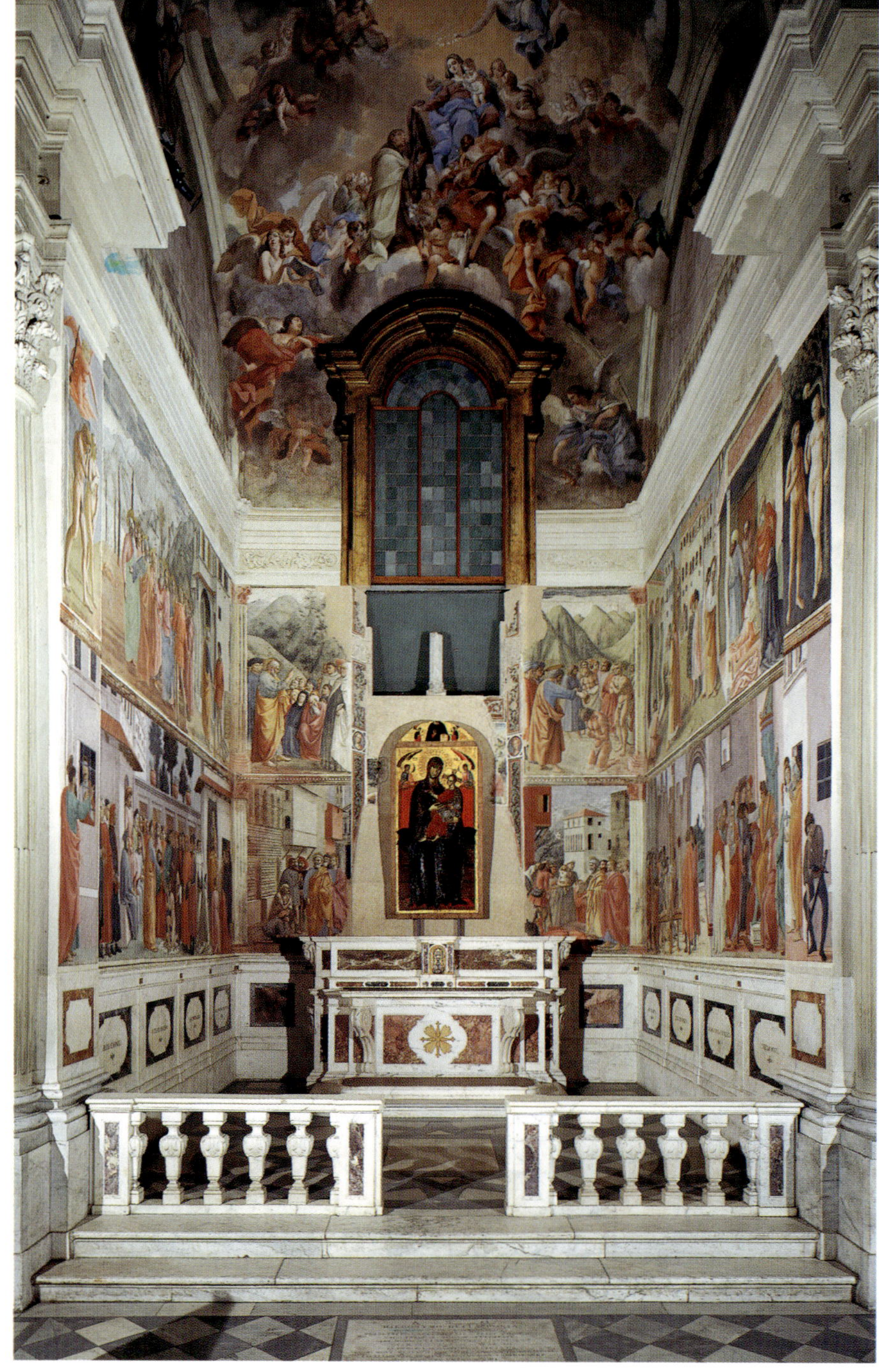

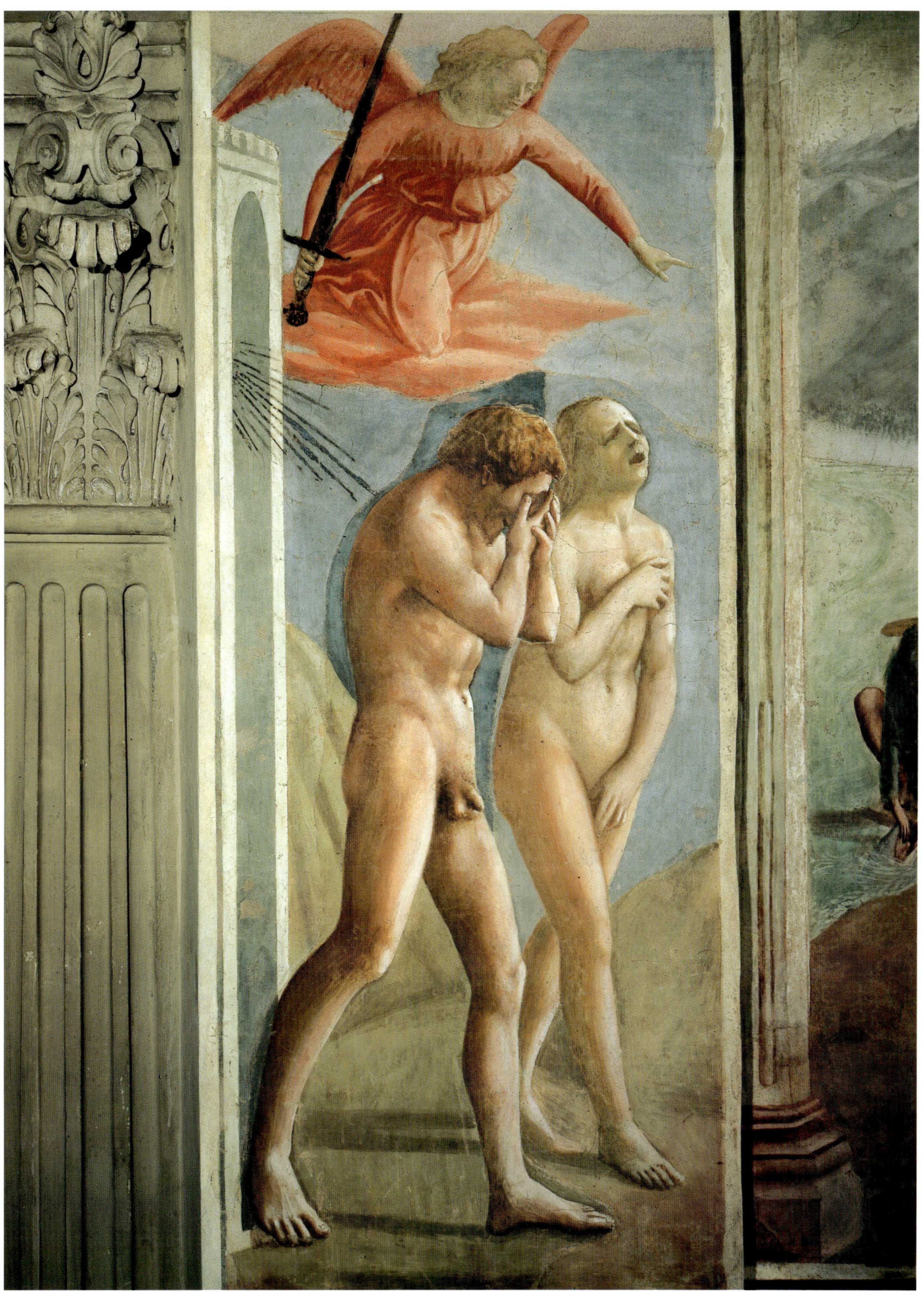

The calling of Peter and Andrew. The introduction of the scene depicting Adam and Eve has instead been explained by the Carmelites' involvement in the programme and their desire for a representation of Original Sin as against St Peter, whose religious rather than political vision they preferred to underline, of the possibility of redemption from sin. However, the non-inclusion of the scene, central to this vision, of the "Denial", goes against that interpretation. The loss of numerous passages also makes clearer understanding of the work stages difficult. It is generally thought that at the beginning only Masolino was on the scaffolding, and to him is due vault and large lunettes. The later entry of Masaccio, who joined him at the level of the second order (originally the central register, that had the most significant scenes from the iconological point of view), demonstrates in any case the absolutely identical, and indeed symmetrical, import of the two artists. Of what remains of the original lower register, it seems to have been taken ahead only by Masaccio on the left wall. In suggesting a date one has to take into account the termini of the beginning of the partnership between the two artists (end of 1423-beginning of 1424), Masolino's departure for Hungary (September 1425), the almost continuous presence in Pisa of Masaccio in 1426, his departure for Rome (July 1427).

The reception by the Florentine artistic community of the novelty in the chapel was immense and immediate. Vasari recounts that a young monastery converse who would himself become a painter, Filippo Lippi, "frequented it every day for his amusement, and here exercising himself continuously in the company of many young men who were always drawing, he advanced in skill and knowledge far beyond the others".

For succeeding generations the frequenting of the Brancacci became a veritable school of election: "all the most celebrated sculptors and painters that there have been since him to now, by exercising themselves and studying in this chapel, have become excelling and famous", Leonardo, Michelangelo and Raphael among them, "and in short all those who have sought to learn that art, went to learn always to this chapel, and grasp the precepts and the rules of Masaccio's fine making of figures".

The work broke off for reasons unknown and incomprehensible in terms of the customs of the time and of the work rhythms necessary for the completion of the cycle. In fact Felice Brancacci's will of 1432 speaks of the unfinished decoration. An opponent of the Medici, in 1435 Felice was exiled from Florence and declared himself a rebel in 1458. The decoration of the chapel then suffered an abysmal episode of *damnatio memoriae* in the scenes of the lower register where members of the Brancacci family, and anti-Medici group linked with them, were depicted. The family was prevented from concerning itself with the chapel which, to erase the memory of a patronage that had become an embarrassment, was dedicated to the Madonna del Popolo, with the transfer here of the thirteenth-century image of the *Madonna*, still visible today on the altar. The decoration of the chapel was made good and completed by Filippino Lippi around 1481-1483, after the ban on the Brancacci was revoked in 1474. Perhaps members of a collateral branch of the family dealt with the task, to earn the goodwill of the Medici regime and make plain their distance from their

Facing page:
The tribute
(whole and detail)
fresco
247 x 597;
c. 1424-1426

On pages 52-53:
The resurrection of the son of Theophilus and St Peter in cathedra
(whole and detail)
fresco
247 x 588;
c. 1424-1426

On page 54:
St Peter healing the sick with his shadow
fresco
232 x 162;
c. 1424-1426

On page 55:
The bestowing of alms and the death of Ananias
(whole and detail)
fresco
232 x 157;
c. 1424-1426

The baptism of the neophytes
fresco
247 x 172
c. 1424-1426

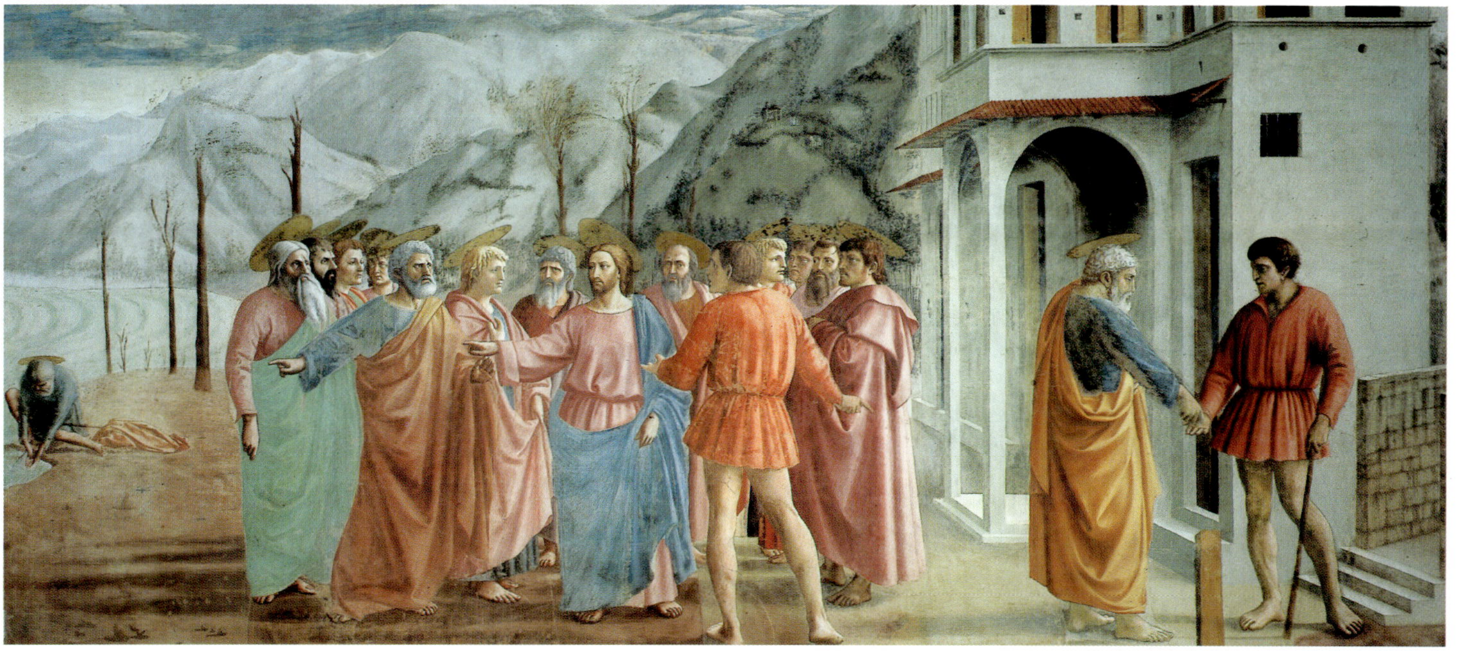

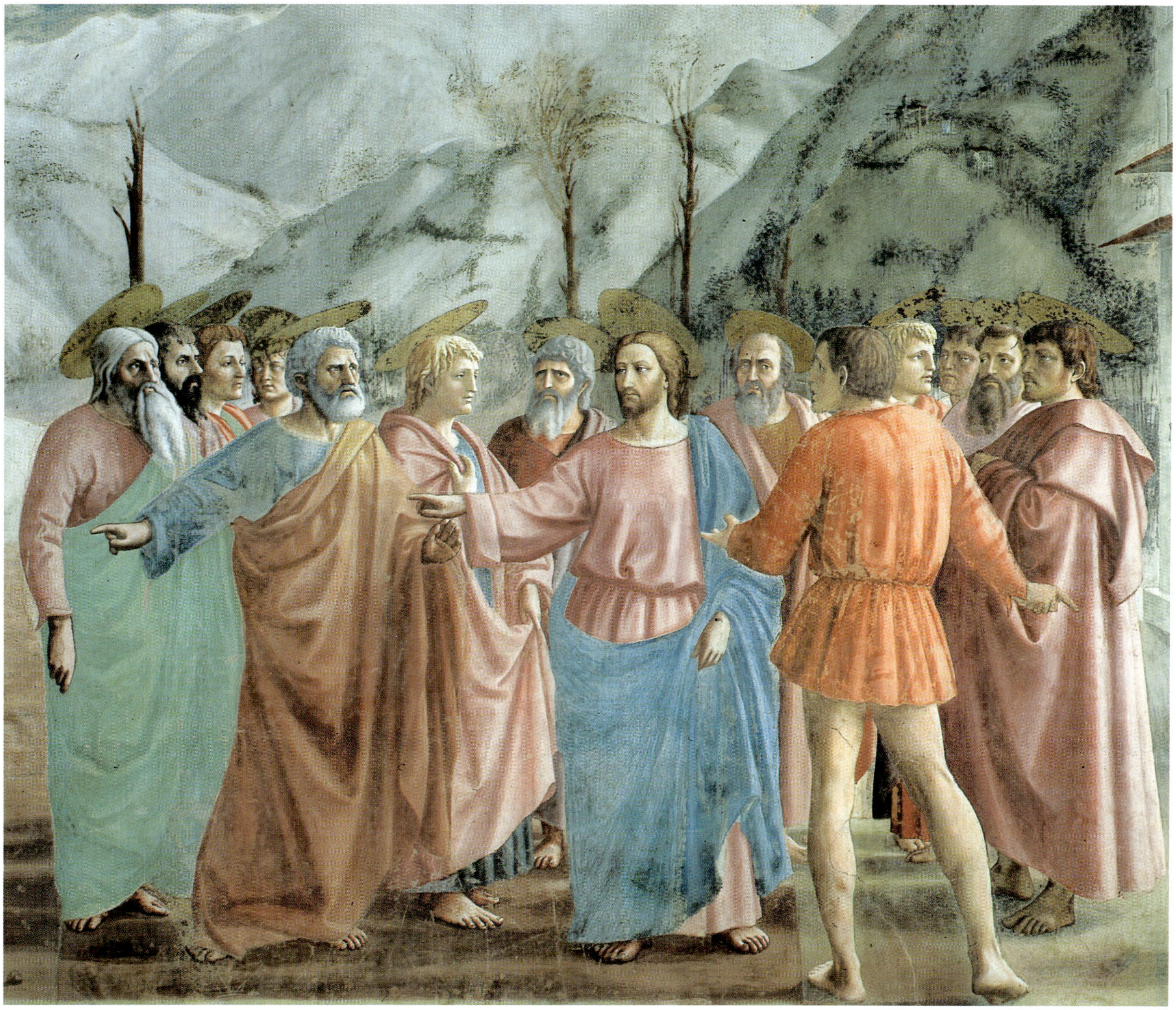

exiled kin. The chapel seems to have passed in definitive fashion to the Carmelites until, on the 17th of July, the Marchese Ferroni tried to take possession of it and destroy the frescoes. Their fame and the concern of the Grand Duchess Vittoria della Rovere ("either she did it on her own initiative, or incited by the Academy of the Painters", according to the Carmelite Benedetto Ricci), while for the friars "anything would have been better than seeing those snouts dressed in ancient fashion with smocks and long cloaks".

Between 1746 and 1748 work was undertaken which led among other things to the disastrous destruction of the frescoes of the vault and lunettes, "because the figures in the third order had nothing of worth". In their place Vincenzo Meucci painted scenes of Carmelite devotion, with the collaboration of the perspective painter Carlo Sacconi. In 1771, finally, the frescoes were rescued from the fire that almost completely destroyed the church thanks to the providential restoration financed by the Grand Duke of Tuscany.

In the upper order the painting cycle starts from *The temptation of Adam and Eve*, the work of Masolino. The second square, in a thematic reading, must be considered *The expulsion from Paradise* by Masaccio. Then follow *The tribute*, painted by Masaccio (which might refer to the quarrel about financial reform going on in those years in Florence), *The preaching of St Peter* by Masolino, *The baptism of the neophytes* by Masaccio and *The healing of the lame and the resurrection of Tabitha* by Masolino. In the lower register are the scenes *St Peter in prison visited by St Paul* by Filippino Lippi, *The resurrection of the son of Theophilus*, painted by Masaccio but damaged by the *damnatio memoriae* and finished by Filippino, *St Peter in cathedra* by Masaccio, *St Peter healing the sick with his shadow* by Masaccio, *The bestowing of alms and the death of Ananias* by Masaccio, *The dispute of Simon Magus and the crucifixion of St Peter* by Filippino Lippi; finally *The angel liberating St Peter from prison* by Filippino. That the planning of the whole cycle took place at one time and results from the conception of a tried and tested team like that of the "compagnia" between Masaccio and Masolino is demonstrated by the perfect and balanced alternation between the two artists. Some shared choices were made, consisting of the perspective schema, the framing with classical grooved pilaster strips with Corinthian capitals, the distances and settings that succeed in softening the formal break between one scene and the next. This enormous effort to achieve a harmonic result is particularly evident despite the uncertainties in attribution that have marked the critical history of the chapel particularly as regard passages such as the head of Christ in the *Tribute* or the city background in the *Resurrection of Tabitha*.

The Brancacci marks the coming together of Masaccio and Donatello in a most particular way.

The Brunelleschi influence in the *Trinity* is here left behind in favour of a less maniacal perspective framing, fitting the needs of narrative.

The dramatic and oratorical quality of the scenes and the great simplification of the depictions, free of any superfluous ornament, remind one of Giotto, the inescapable formal and compositional reference point.

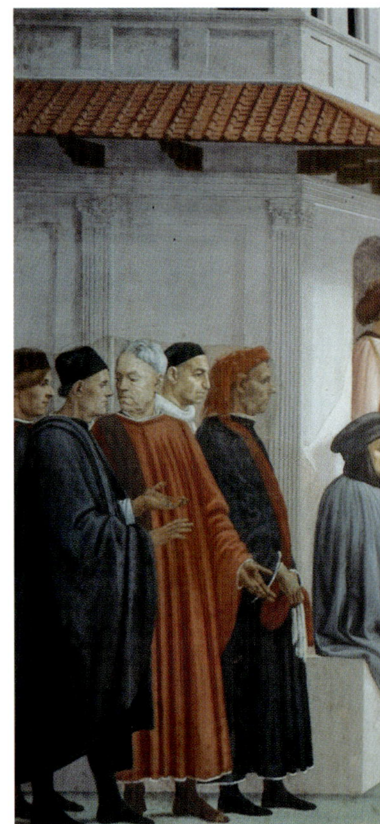

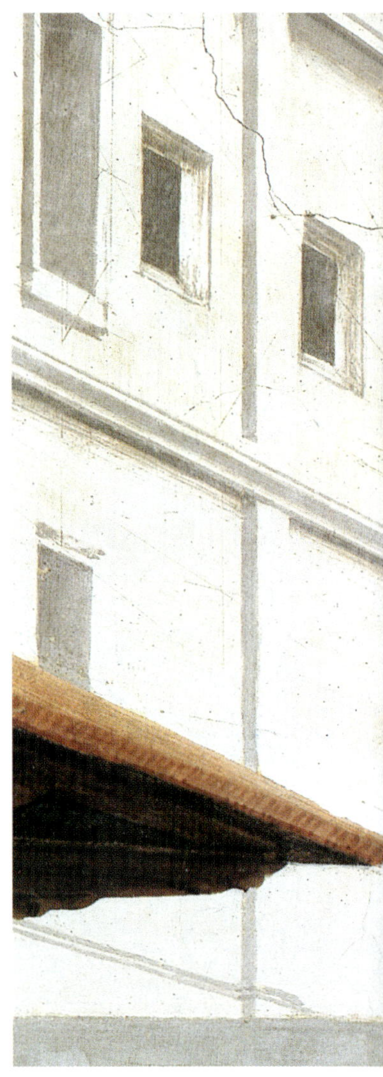

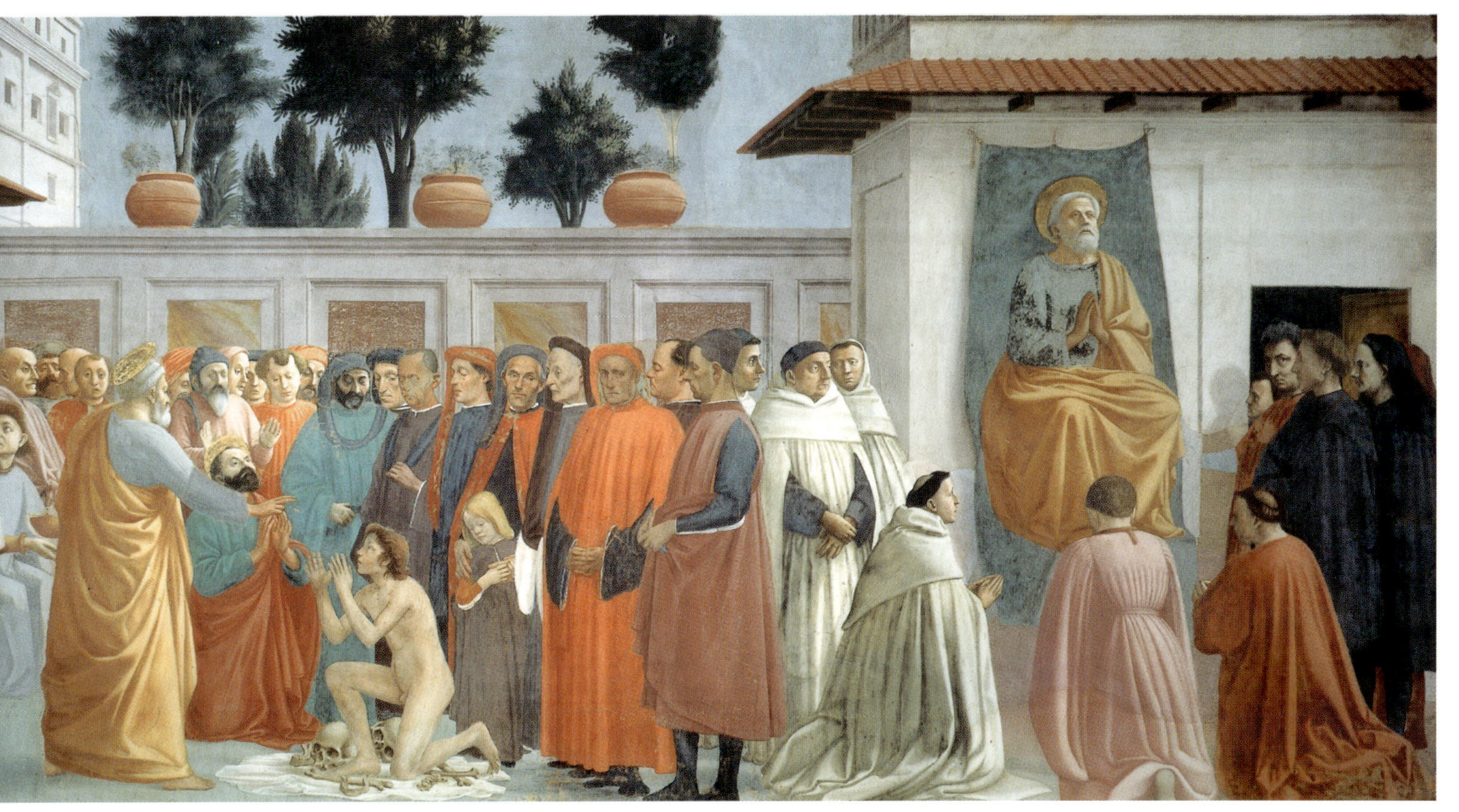

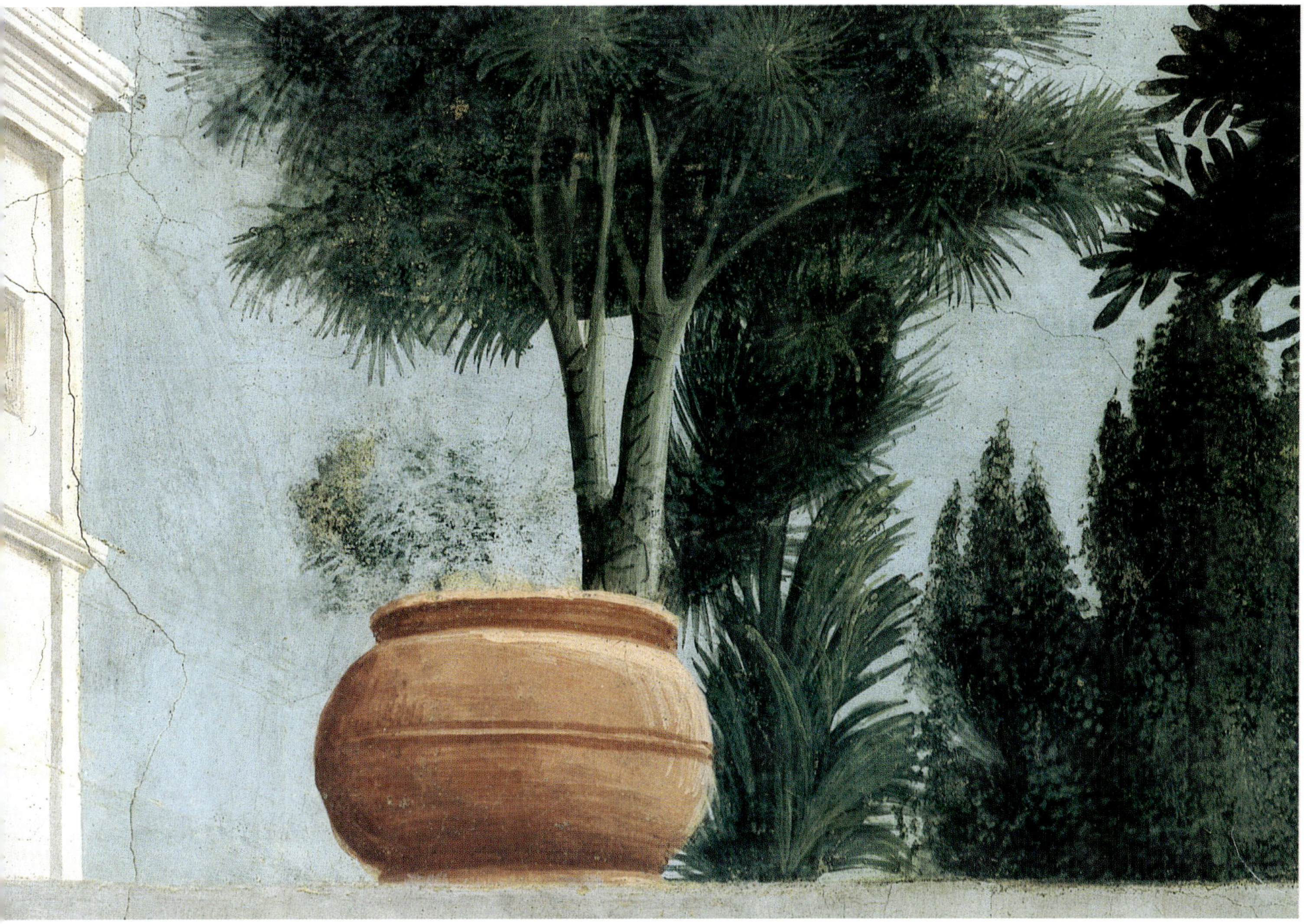

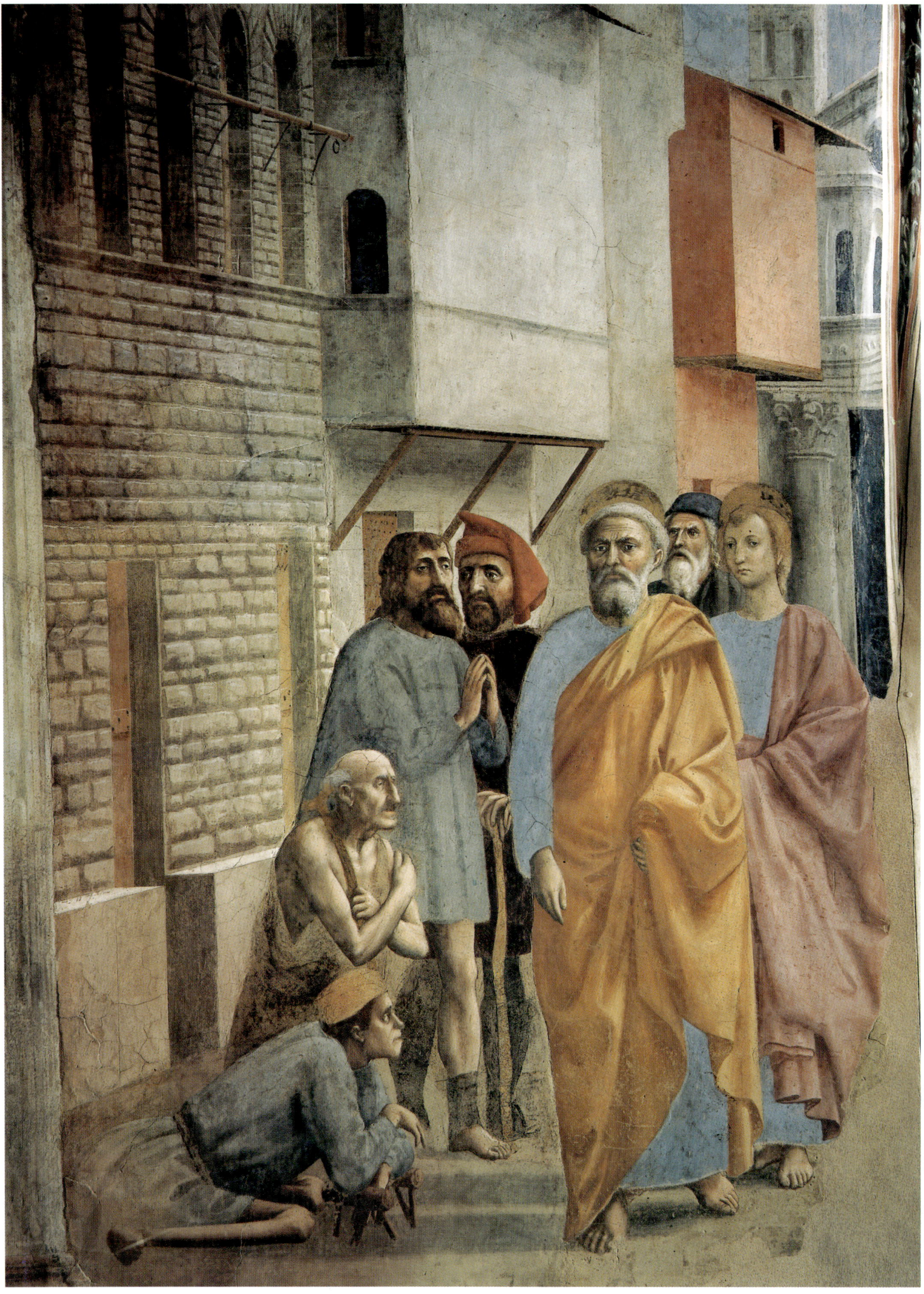

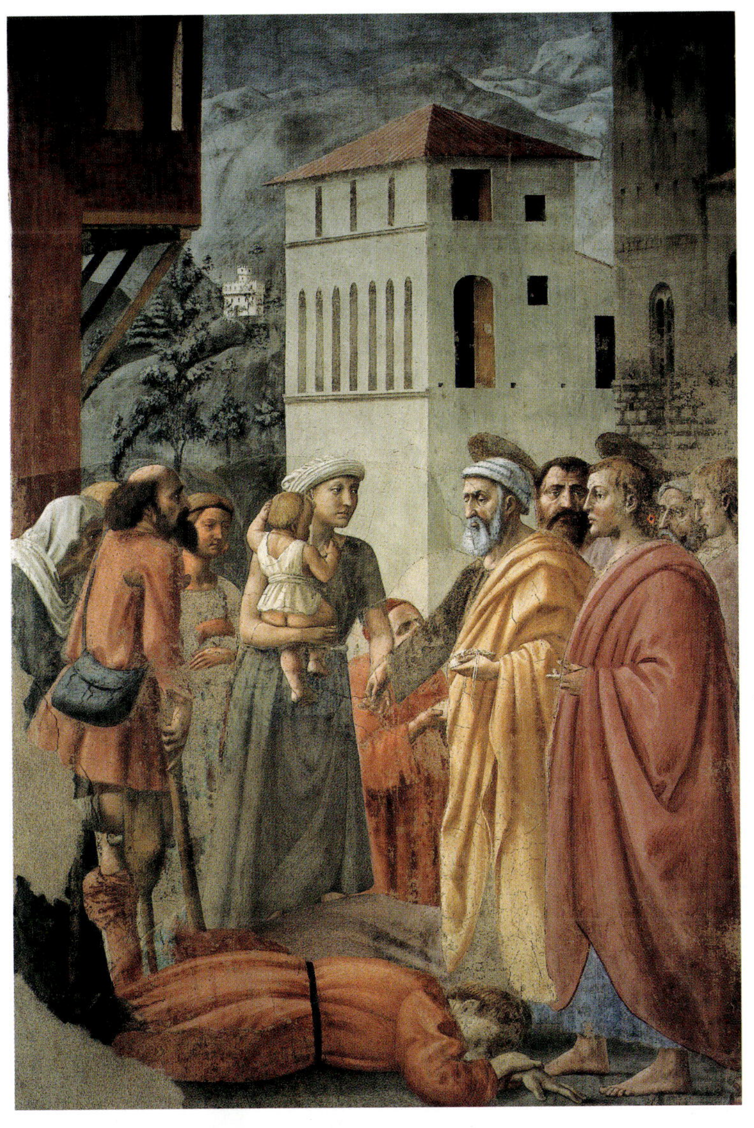

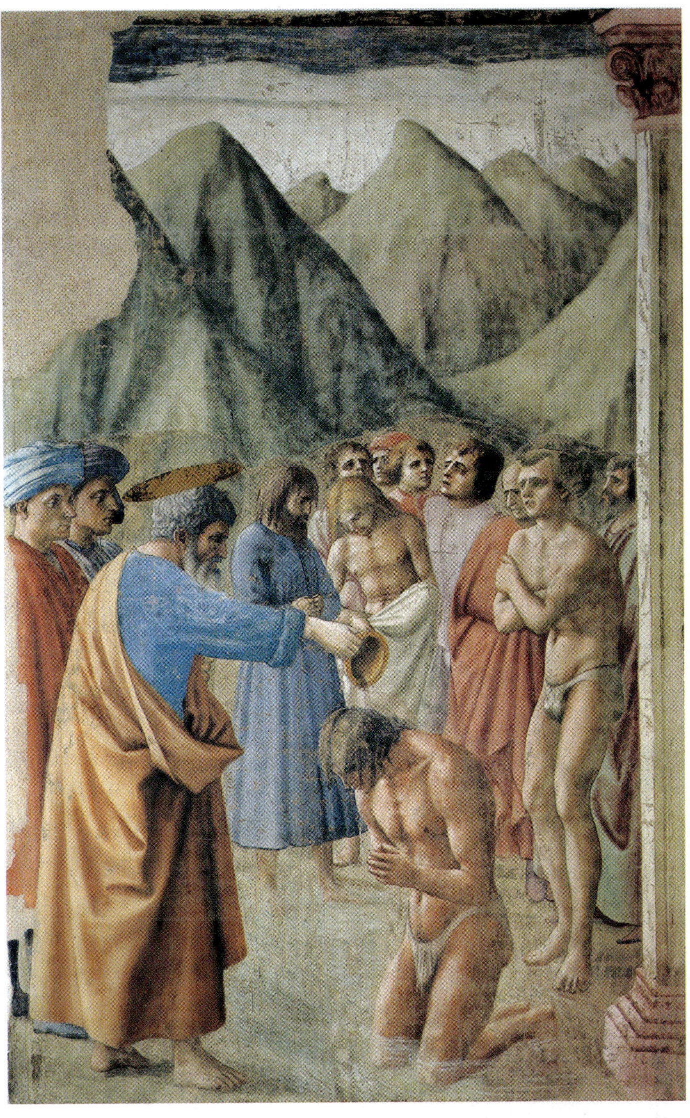

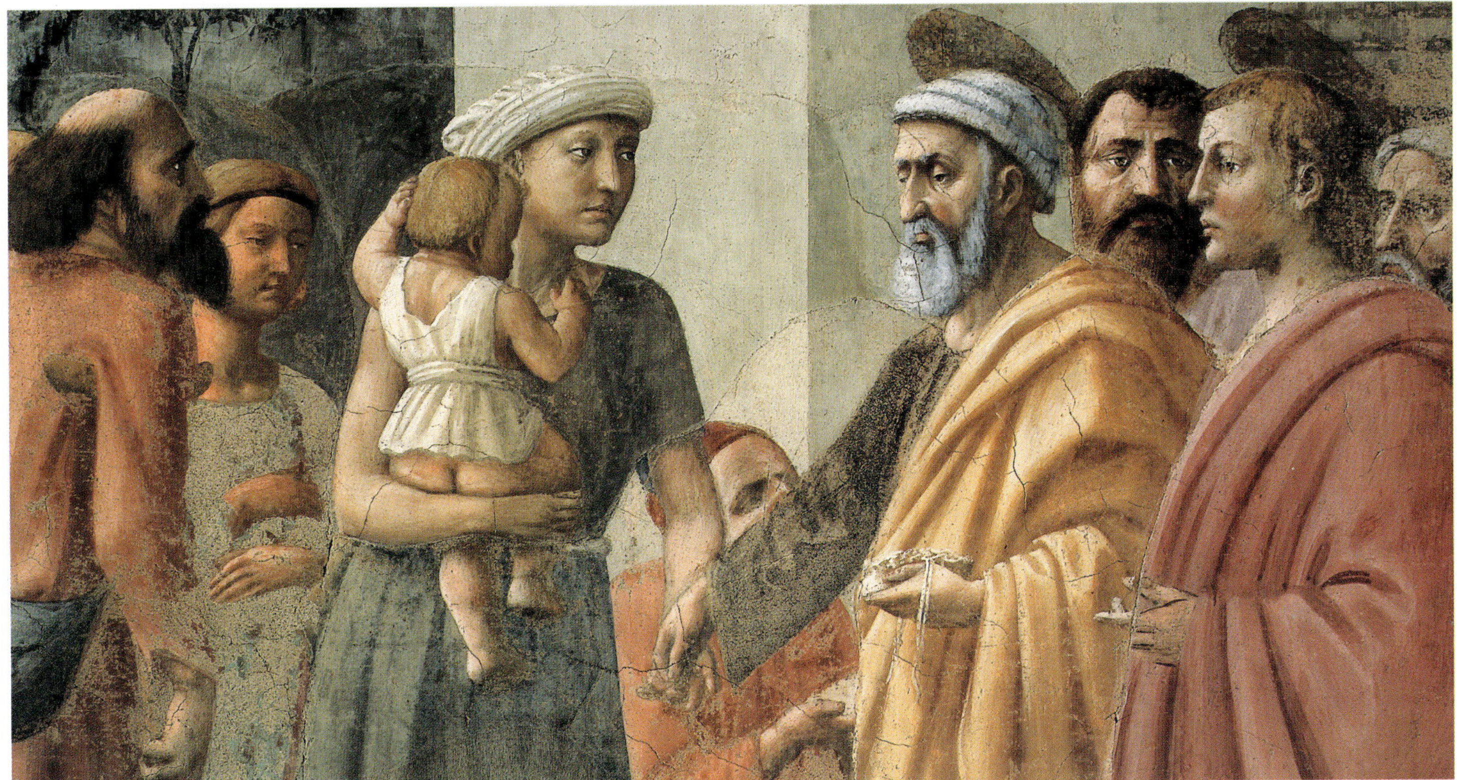

PISA POLYPTYCH

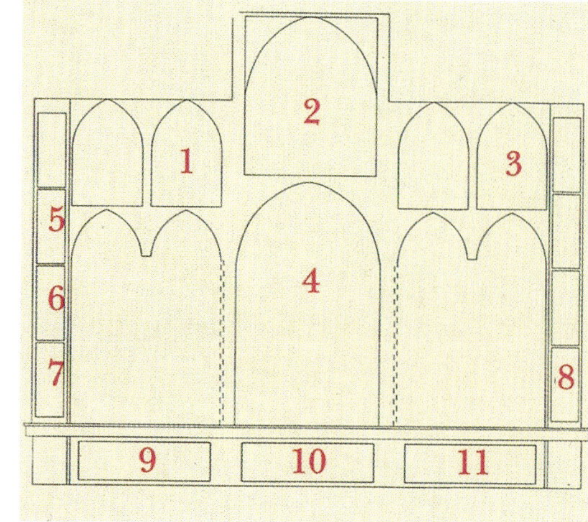

After Masolino's departure for Hungary, in September 1425, Masaccio produced the only work dated and credited to him by the documents, the polyptych (now dismembered) for a chapel in the chancel of the church of the Carmine in Pisa. Scattered through various museums, only four main pieces more or less certain survive (the *Madonna with Child,* the *Crucifixion,* the *St Paul* and the *St Andrew*); three elements of the altarpiece and four small saints on the pilasters. The wealth of documentation that has come down to us since the making of the polyptych results from to the profession of the person who commissioned it, the notary Giuliano di Colino degli Scarsi: many of the relative papers were collected by him and copied from the originals to make a notebook of the expenses for the building and decoration of the family chapel. The actual engagement contract with Masaccio has not come down to us, but the sequence of operations which the patron committed himself to seems clear enough. To the woodworker Antonio di Biagio 18 florins were paid for the wooden structure of the altarpiece. The first reference to Masaccio came immediately after: "he painted it, beginning on the 19th of February 1426". There is no suggestion of Masaccio's being involved with the wooden structure, a custom common enough with painters between the fourteenth and fifteenth century. Except in rare cases, the structure of the polyptych resulted from the patron's decision or from the way it was to fit into the general decoration of the church. In Pisa, with Masaccio, were Andrea di Giusto and Lo Scheggia, along with other painters (at least a third painter who executed the *Stories of St Julian and St Nicholas*). The payments, made in several instalments, are rather interesting. On as many as two occasions Donatello occurs, evidently linked to Masaccio. The payment of October 1426, at which Masaccio was not present, is significant: the notary demanded and received by means of a legal contract a promise that the painter would not do "other work before this is finished". Lo Scheggia and a Pisan sculptor, who received the instalment, were required to act as guarantors to a penal clause of 100 florins, an extremely high figure that allows one to suppose a concrete possibility that Masaccio might devote himself to other work. On 26 December 1426, in the chapter house of the Carmine in Pisa, the remainder of the sum agreed was paid. But the *Polyptych* was still not finished: Ser Giuliano stipulated a reserve with Masaccio "that he must con-

Reconstruction of the *Pisa Polyptych* (Berti-Foggi 1989):
1. *St Paul* (Pisa, San Matteo National Museum)
2. *Crucifixion* (Naples, Capodimonte Museum)
3. *St Andrew* (Malibu, J. Paul Getty Museum)
4. *Enthroned Madonna and Child with four angels* (London, National Gallery)
5-8. *St Augustine, St Jerome and two Carmelite Saints* (Berlin, Staatliche Museen)
9-11. *Martyrdom of St Peter and St John the Baptist, Adoration of the Magi, Stories of St Julian and St Nicholas* (Berlin, Staatliche Museen).

Facing page:
Enthroned Madonna and Child with four angels
tempera on wood 135.5 x 73; 1426 London, National Gallery

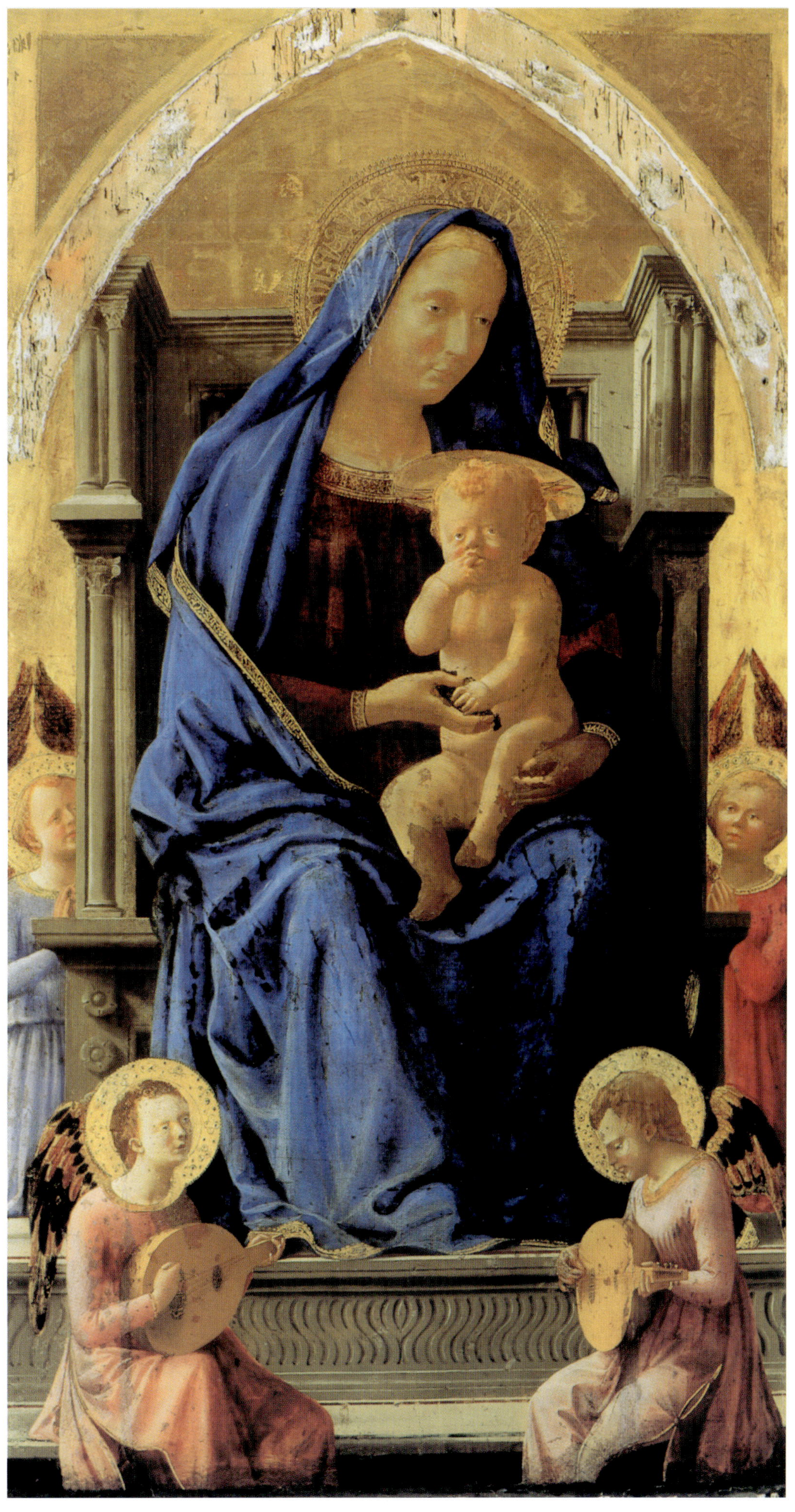

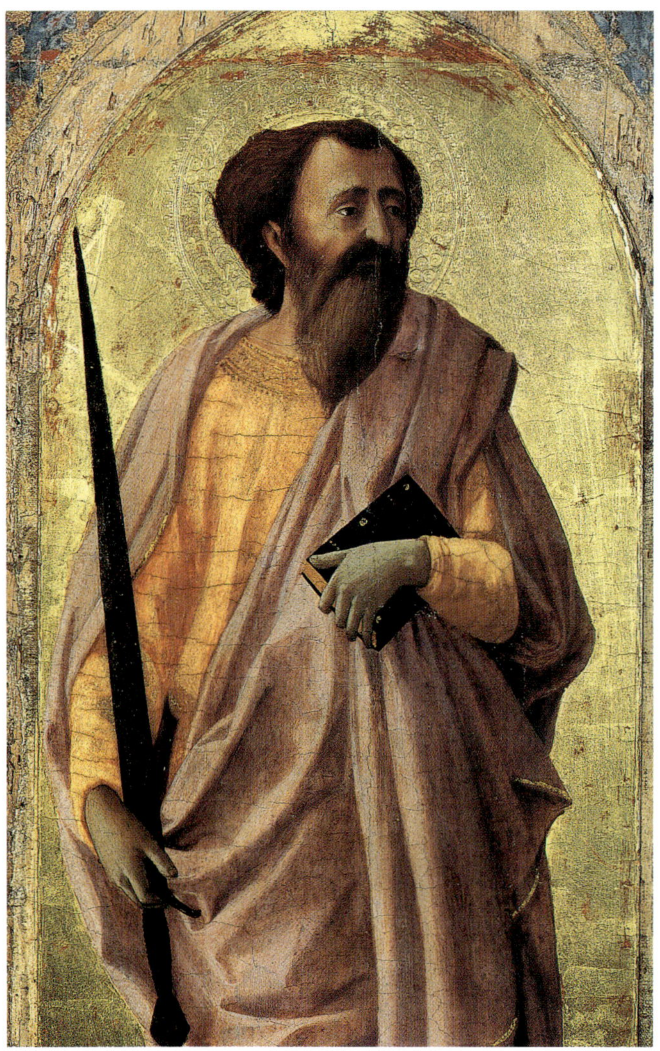

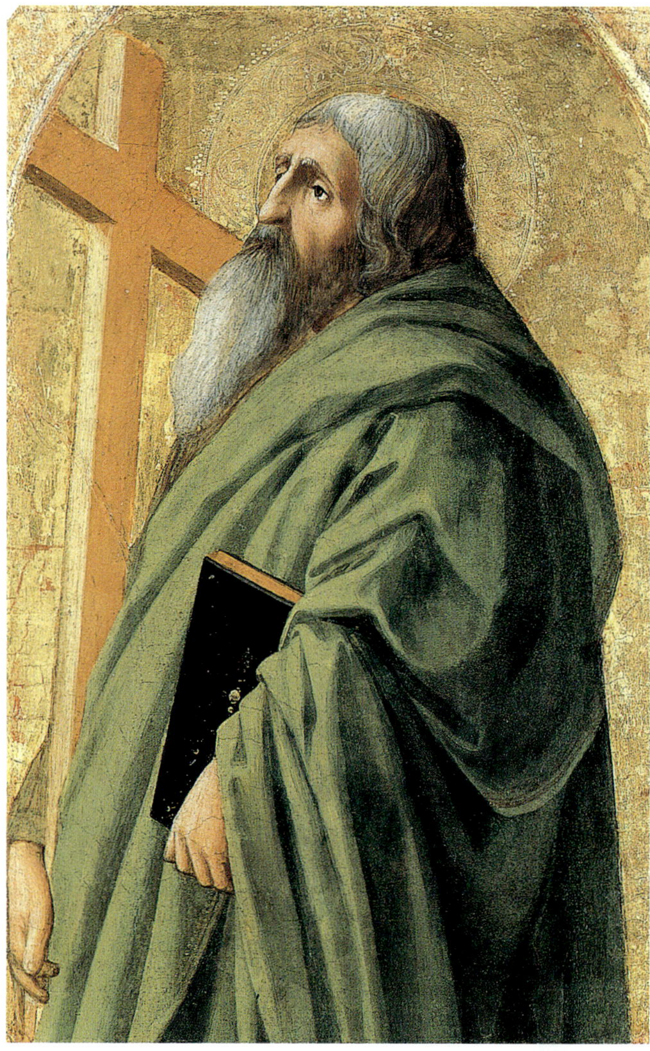

sign my panel finished". The appointment of the prior as evaluator of the work leads one to suggest the iconographic-iconological aspect, as illustration of a specific religious message, had great importance. The spacing of the instalments with which the *Polyptych* was paid over the span of a year also seems to suggest that the work was interrupted at various times. Given a pre-existing wooden structure, the time technically required to complete a work of the (presumed) dimensions and complexity of the *Polyptych*, with work going on at the same time in the workshop, should not have been so long. That the stage of working out the image was unusually uncertain for Masaccio is made clear by the investigations carried out on the main panels. The *Crucifixion* underwent various changes in the course of work, probably for reasons other the artist's indecision (a request from the patron?). The structure of the Cross was to have a panel with an inscription, then replaced by the tree with the pelican. The insertion of the figure of the Magdalen also dates from this stage. The iconography thus chosen was rich in soteriological motifs as against that proposed by Masaccio: from the pelican that gashes its breast to feed its young, to the sacrifice of the Cross, linked by that same blood, to the Eucharistic sacrifice (the bunch of grapes in the Child's hand). The investigation also reveals reworking of the Virgin in the main section at various times and at different stages of work. A change in the image due perhaps to the constraint Masaccio must

St Paul
tempera on wood
58.5 x 33.5
Pisa, San Matteo
National Museum

St Andrew
tempera on wood
52.3 x 32
Malibu, J. Paul Getty
Museum

Facing page:
Crucifixion
tempera on wood
82.1 x 63.5
Naples, Capodimonte
Museum

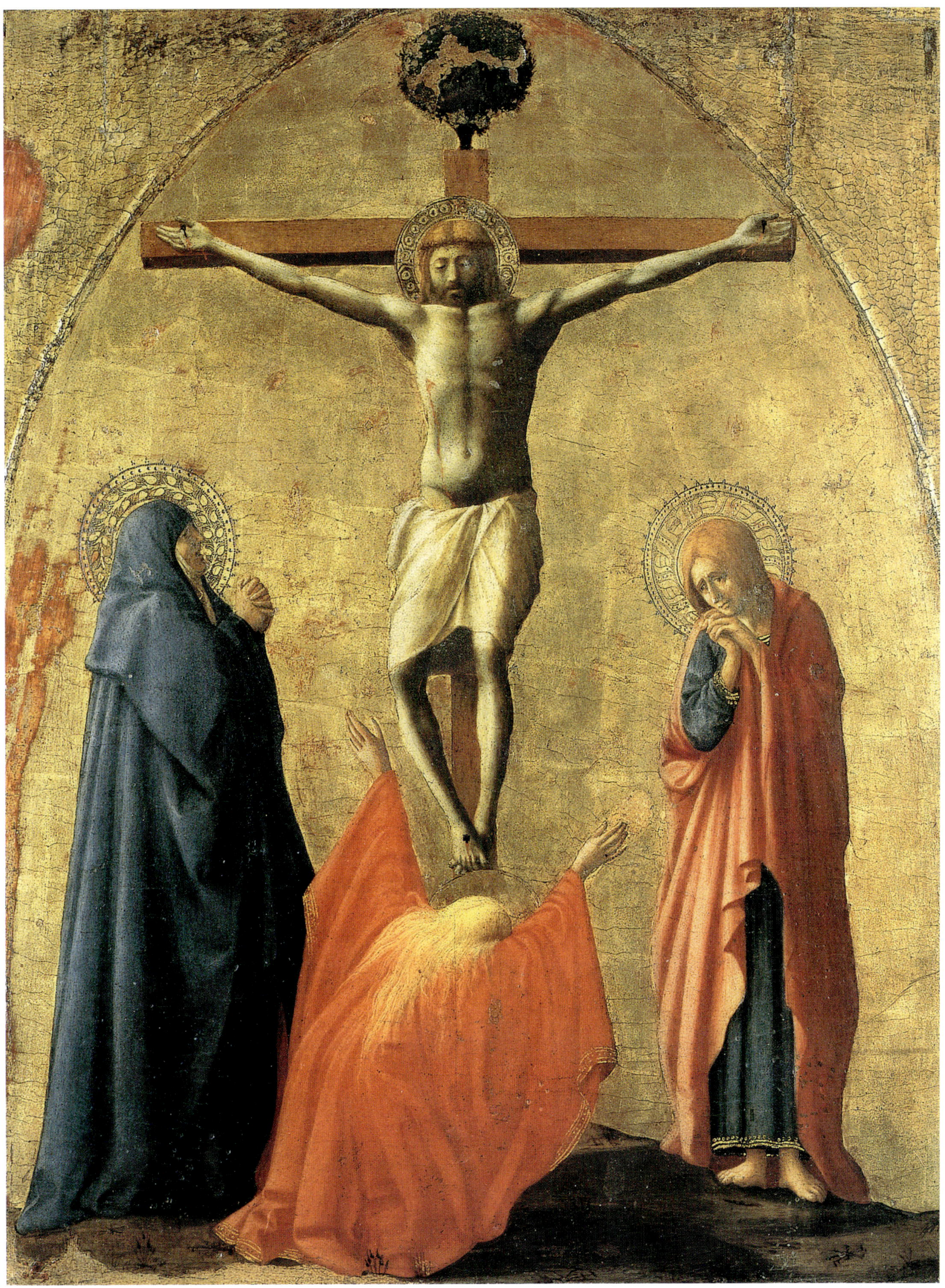

have felt in working in a predetermined field: instead of reducing his figures, the artist took the aesthetic decision of emphasising their constriction within the limits set. This is the reason for the trimming of the top of the throne, the side angels relegated to a narrow space between the throne and the end of the panel, the elimination of part of the angel musicians' legs, the emphasis on the body mass of the Virgin. Recent scientific investigation leads one to suggest that the *St Paul* and the *St Andrew* did not belong to the original complex: the panels, without doubt matching, betray marks of construction relating to the putting-on of the preparatory layers and of gilding that fit ill with the rest of the polyptych. Great "altar machines", polyptychs were in fact constructed according to a rigid structural logic deriving from precise workshop traditions and precise requirements of solidity. In the construction practice of polyptychs in the fourteenth and fifteenth-century Tuscan milieu, the various sections were joined together at the back by a system of horizontal cross-battens that served to hold, support and link the structure. These were running pieces wich stretched the length of the whole structure, hence panels belonging to the same polyptych have to be of identical width and show aligned traces of the cross-battens (removed in dismantling, but heads of the nails used often remain embedded in the panels). In the case of the two supposed pinnacle panels, the thickness of the panels does not correspond to that of the central part of the polyptych. Added to this, the nail holes of the cross-battens system do not, on the different components, match up and do not therefore make coherent reconstruction possible. The *Madonna*,

the *Crucifixion*, the elements of the pilasters and of the altarpiece share a common thickness of wood, absolutely that of the original, and the same traces of tools on the back, again original. Furthermore the *Madonna* and the *Crucifixion* were originally painted on a single continuous board. Whereas on the *St Andrew* and on the *St Paul* X-radiograph has revealed perfectly compatible nail holes from cross-battens. Though separated by the central elements of a polyptych, the two panels must have belonged to a single but independent polyptych. And it is impossible to connect the cross-battens of the structure composed by the *Madonna* and *Crucifixion* with those of the cusps. Close scrutiny of the upper edges of the *St Paul*, furthermore, reveals traces of the original construction in which the arch was not cusped, but round, a further element that differentiates it from the other panels of the polyptych.

Masaccio may therefore have made a second polyptych for the Carmine (given the indubitable provenance of the *St Paul*), as confirmed by the documented relation between the artist and the Del Podio, another family that had patronage of an altar in the Carmine. In January 1427 Masaccio was in fact witness to a notarial deed, drafted by Ser Giuliano, regarding the cession by the Del Podio to the Carmelites of a chapel adjacent to the large one in exchange for the sacristy. The second Pisan polyptych, smaller in size, to which the panels with the two saints will have belonged, may have been made for the Del Podio. The silence of the old sources, Vasari first of all, on this work may be explained by the fact that, at the time of the *Lives*, it had already been removed from the chapel and dismembered.

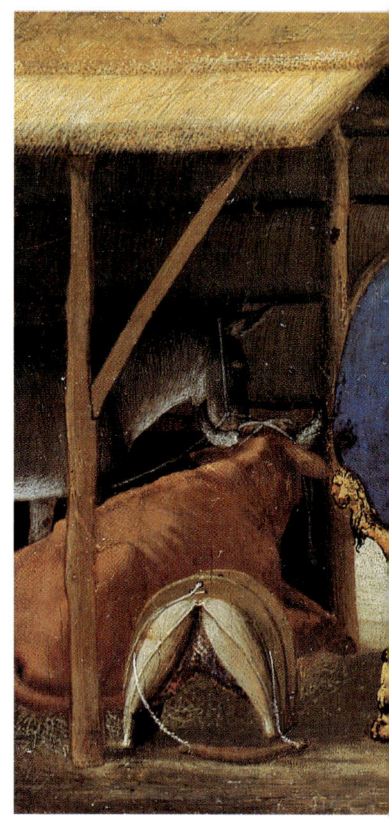

*Adoration
of the Magi*
tempera on wood
21 x 61
Berlin, Staatliche
Museen

*Martyrdom
of St Peter
and St John
the Baptist*
tempera on wood
21 x 61
Berlin, Staatliche
Museen

*Stories of St Julian
and St Nicholas*
tempera on wood
21 x 61
Berlin, Staatliche
Museen

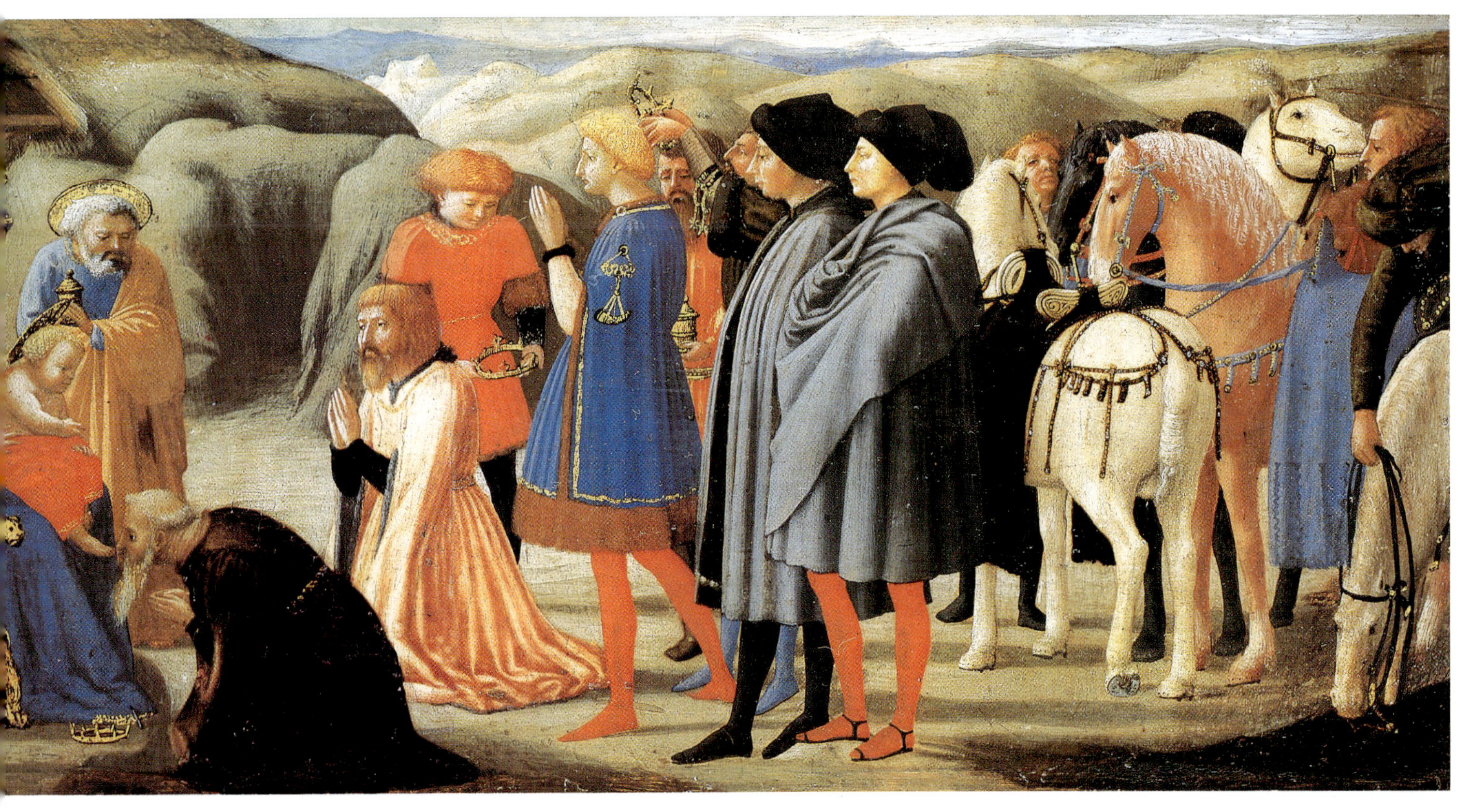

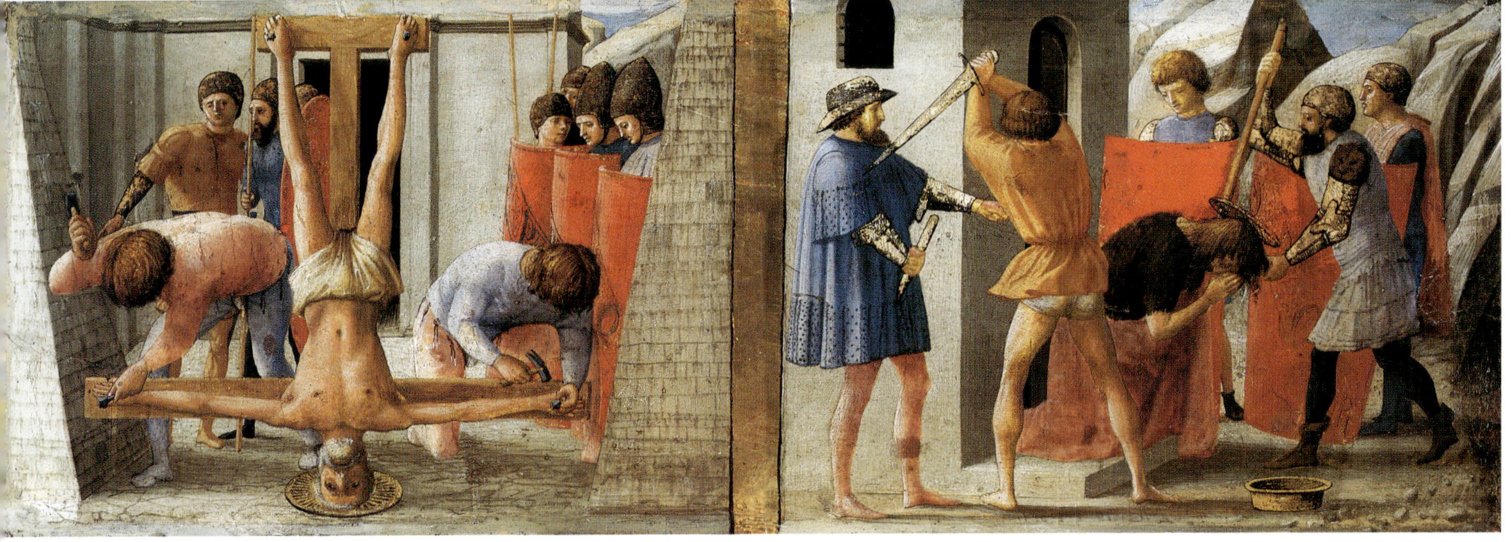

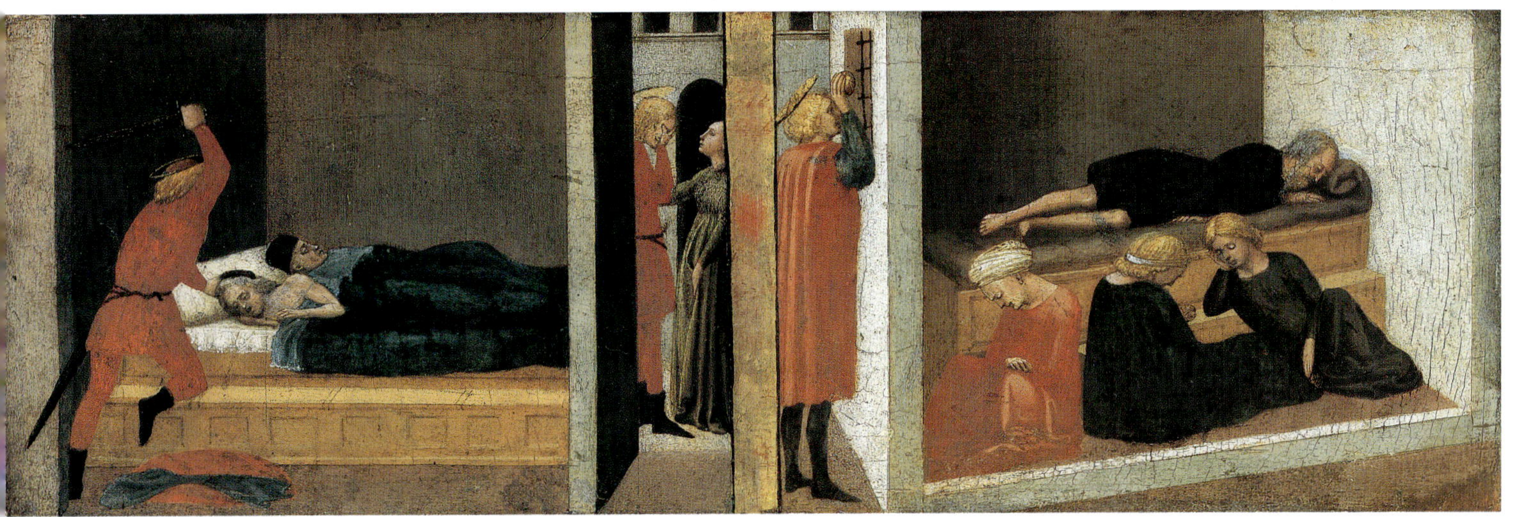

INDEX OF NAMES AND WORKS
Numbers in italic refer to illustrations and their captions.

Alberti, Leon Battista, *5*
Alessandra, sister of Masaccio, 4
Andrea di Giusto Manzini, 8, 56
Antonio di Biagio, 56

Barberino di Mugello, 4
Berenson, Bernard, 11
Berlin, Staatliche Museen, *30-31, 60-61*
Berti, Luciano, 44
Bicci di Lorenzo, 6-7
  Enthroned Madonna and Child and a donor, 9
Boni, family, *21*
Brancacci, family, 30, 48-50
  Felice, 48-50
Bremen, Kunsthalle, *21*
Brunelleschi, Filippo, *5*, 10-17, 30, 40, 44, 46, 52

Cairo, 48
Carnesecchi, family, 20-21
Carocci, Guido, 44
Cascia di Reggello, church of San Pietro, *15, 44-47*
Casini, Antonio, cardinal, 34
Castiglione Olona, 19, 40
Caterina, daughter of Tedesco di Feo, 6
Cennini, Cennino, 8, 26
Colonna, family (*see also* Martin V), 36

Della Rovere, Vittoria, Grand Duchess, 52
Del Podio, family, 60
Domenico Veneziano, *Madonna of Humility*, 32
Donatello (Donato di Niccolò di Betto Bardi), 11,
  38, 44, 46, *47*, 52, 56
  St George, 11, *12*
  St George freeing the princess, 11, *13*

Empoli, Museum of the Collegiata, *9*
  Santo Stefano degli Agostiniani, 20

Farnese, collection, 37
Ferroni, Marchese, 52
Florence, 4, 6, 7, 8, 9, 10-16, 18, 19, 20, 22, *24*, 30,
  32, 34, 36, *39*, 40, 46, 48, 50, 52
  Accademia Gallery, *31*
  Badia Fiorentina, 10, 13
  Baptistery, 19
  Bargello Museum, *12, 13*
  Cestello Archiepiscopal Museum, *21*
  Dome (Santa Maria del Fiore), 10-11, 16, *24*
  Giotto's Campanile, 11
  Horne Museum, *22, 23*
  Orsanmichele, 11, *12, 13*
  Santa Maria del Carmine, Brancacci Chapel, *5, 7,
  18, 19, 26, 27, 28, 29*, 30, 32, *48-55*
  Santa Maria Maggiore, 21

Santa Maria Novella, 14, *16-17*
Sant'Ambrogio, 24
Spedale degli Innocenti, 10
Uffizi Gallery, *11, 24, 25, 34, 35*
Francesco d'Antonio, painter, 21

Ghiberti, Lorenzo, 11, 19
Giotto, 11, 46, 52
Giovanni di Mone d'Andreuccio, father of Masaccio,
  4-5, 9, 12
Giovanni di ser Giovanni, brother of Masaccio, *see*
  Lo Scheggia
Giovenale di Narni, saint, 46
Giuliano di Colino degli Scarsi, 56, 58, 60
Gualtieri di Brienne (Duke of Athens), *24*

Hungary, 18, 27, 30-32, 34, 50, 56

Jacopa di Martinozzo di Dino, mother
  of Masaccio, 4-9

Leonardo da Vinci, 50
Leopoldo I, Grand Duke of Tuscany, 52
Liborius III, Pope, 36
Lippi, Filippino, *26, 27*, 50, 52
  The angel liberating St Peter from prison, 52
  *The dispute of Simon Magus and the crucifixion
  of St Peter*, 52
  St Peter in prison visited by St Paul, 52
Lippi, Filippo, 50
Livorno, 48
London, National Gallery, *33, 37, 39, 41, 57*
Longhi, Roberto, 11, 26
Lorenzetti, Ambrogio, 16
Lorenzo Monaco (Pietro di Giovanni), 10, *11*
  Coronation of the Virgin, 11
Lucca, 46

Malibu, J. Paul Getty Museum, *58*
Manetti, Antonio, 13, 14
Mariotto di Cristofano, 6
  Christus patiens between the Virgin and St Lucy, 9
Martin V (Oddone Colonna), Pope, 34, 36
Masaccio
  Brancacci Chapel, 16, 20, *26, 27*, 30, 32, *48-55*
  The baptism of the neophytes, 29, 52, 55
  *The bestowing of alms and the death
  of Ananias*, 52, *55*
  *The expulsion of Adam and Eve from
  Paradise*, 22, *49*, 50, 52
  *The healing of the lame and the resurrection
  of Tabitha, 19*, 52
  The resurrection of the son of Teophilus, 52-53
  *St Peter healing the sick with his shadow, 7,
  18*, 52, *54*
  St Peter in cathedra, 5, 18, 28, 52-53
  The tribute, 7, 51, 52
  Carnesecchi Triptych, 21-24, 29

Scenes from the legend of St Julian, 22, 23, 24
Colonna Polyptych (see also Masolino), 36-40
  St Jerome and St John the Baptist, 37, 39, 41
Madonna and Child (Madonna del Solletico), 34, 35
Madonna of Humility (attr., see Domenico
  Veneziano), 32
Pisa Polyptych, 16, 33, *56-61*
  Adoration of the Magi, 60-61
  Crucifixion 58, *59*
  *Enthroned Madonna and Child with
  four angels, 33, 57*, 58, 60
  *Martyrdom of St Peter and St John
  the Baptist, 61*
  St Andrew, 58, 60
  St Paul, 58, 60
  Stories of St Julian and St Nicholas, 56, *61*
Sagra del Carmine (lost), 30
San Giovenale Triptych, 6, 12, 13-14, *15*, 16, 18,
  23, *44-47*
St Anne Metterza, 24-25, 26-29
St Yves of Brittany with his pupils, 13
Trinity, 14-16, 16-17, 52
Masaccio, workshop of, *Birthing-stool, 30-31, 32-33*
  Liberation of the possessed man, 32
Masolino da Panicale (Tommaso di Cristoforo
di Fino), 5, *18*, 19-33, 34-40, 48-52, 56
  Brancacci Chapel (see also Masaccio), 16, 20,
  30, 32, 48-55
  The boat (lost), 48
  The calling of Peter and Andrew (lost), 50
  *The healing of the lame and the resurrection
  of Tabitha, 19*, 52
  The preaching of St Peter, 52
  Temptation of Adam and Eve, 50, 52
  Carnesecchi Triptych (see also Masaccio)
  Madonna and Child, 22, 24
  Scenes of the legend of St Julian, 21-22,
  23, 24
  St Julian, 21, 22, 24
  Colonna Polyptych, 36-40
  Miracle of the Snow, 36-37, 38
  Our Lady of the Assumption, 37, 38
  St Gregory and St Mathias, 37, 38
  St John the Evangelist and St Martin, 37, 38
  St Peter and St Paul, 37, 38, 40
  Madonna of Humility, 21
  St Anne Metterza (see Masaccio)
Medici, family, 50
Meucci, Vincenzo, 52
Michelangelo Buonarroti, 36, 50
Mone d'Andreuccio, grandfather of Masaccio, 4, 8, 46
Montauban, Musée Ingres, *23*

Nanni di Banco, 11
  Four crowned Saints, 12
Naples, Capodimonte Museum, *37, 59*
Narni, 46
Niccolò di ser Lapo, 10, 12

Panicale (Valdarno), 18
Paolo Uccello (Paolo di Dono), 21
Philadelphia, Museum of Art, 33, 37
Pippo Spano (Filippo Scolari), 18-19, 30, 32, 34
Pirez, Alvaro, 10
Pisa, 8, 33, 48, 50, 56-60
   San Matteo National Museum, *58*
   Santa Maria del Carmine, 33, 56-60

Raphael, 50
Ricci, Benedetto, friar, 52
Rome, 19, 34-40, 46, 50
   Saint Peter's in the Vatican, 36, 38-40

Sancta Sanctorum, 36
San Giovanni in Laterano, 36
San Paolo fuori le Mura, 36
Santa Maria Maggiore, 36, *37*, 38-40

Sacconi, Carlo, 52
San Giovanni Valdarno (Castel San Giovanni), 4, 6,
   8, 12, 18, 46
   Museum of Santa Maria delle Grazie, *9*
San Giovenale (Reggello), 10, 20, 44, 46
Lo Scheggia (Giovanni di ser Giovanni), 4-6, *7*,
   8, 32, 56
   Adimari Chest, 31

Birthing-stool, 30-31, 32-33
Scolari, Filippo, *see* Pippo Spano
Starnina, Gherardo, 10, 19
   Madonna of Humility, 11

Tedesco di Maestro Feo, 4, 6, 8-9
Toesca, Pietro, 23
Tommaso di Cristofano, goldsmith, 19
Tommaso di Jacopo, 32

Vasari, Giorgio, 4, 5, *7*, 11, *13*, 14, 18, 19, 21, *29*,
   30, 36, 44, 50, 60

Washington, National Gallery of Art, 32

BIBLIOGRAPHY

Sources: A. Manetti, *Vite di XIV Uomini Singhularii in Firenze dal MCCCC innanzi* (before 1497), in *Operette istoriche*, edited by G. Milanesi, Firenze 1887 (other edition edited by P. Murray, in «The Burlington Magazine», 99 [1957], pp. 330-336); *Il Libro di Antonio Billi* (c. 1506-1530), edited by A. Ficarra, Napoli [w.d.]; *Il Codice Magliabechiano* (c. 1537-1542), edited by C. Frey, Berlin 1892; G. Vasari, *Le Vite de' più eccellenti architetti, pittori e scultori italiani da Cimabue insino a' tempi nostri* (Firenze 1550 and Firenze 1568), edited by G. Milanesi, Firenze 1878-1881, II (*The lives of the Artists*, translated with an introduction and notes by J. Conaway Bondanella and P. Bondanella, Oxford University Press 1991); R. Borghini, *Il Riposo*, Firenze 1584; G. Lomazzo, *Trattato dell'Arte della Pittura*, Milano 1584; F. Bocchi, G. Cinelli, *Le bellezze della città di Firenze*, Firenze 1677; M. Lastri, *Etruria pittrice*, Firenze 1791; L. Lanzi, *Storia pittorica della Italia inferiore*, Firenze 1792; J.A. Crowe, G.B. Cavalcaselle, *A History of Painting in Italy*, London 1864.
Articles: O.H. Giglioli, *Masaccio. Saggio di una bibliografia ragionata*, in «Bollettino del R. Istituto di Archeologia e Storia dell'Arte», 4-5 (1929), pp. 55-101; H. Brockhaus, *Die Brancacci-Kapelle in Florenz*, in «Mitteilungen des Kunsthistorischen Instituts in Florenz», 4 (1930), pp. 160-182; J. Mesnil, *La data della morte di Masaccio*, in «Rivista d'arte», VIII (1912), pp. 31-34; U. Procacci, *Documenti e ricerche sopra Masaccio e la sua famiglia*, in «Rivista d'arte», XIV (1932), pp. 489-503; *L'incendio della chiesa del Carmine del 1771*, in «Rivista d'arte», XIV (1932), pp. 141-232; R. Longhi, *Fatti di Masolino e Masaccio*, in «Critica d'arte», 25-26 (1940), pp. 145-191 (other edition in R. Longhi, *Fatti di Masolino e Masaccio e altri studi sul Quattrocento*, Firenze 1975); U. Procacci, *Sulla cronologia delle opere di Masaccio e di Masolino tra il 1425 e il 1428*, in «Rivista d'arte», XXVIII (1953), pp. 3-55; L. Berti, *Masaccio 1422*, in «Commentari», 2 (1961), pp. 84-107; L. Berti, *Masaccio a San Giovenale a Cascia*, in «Acropoli», 1962, pp. 149-165; M. Meiss, *The altered program of the Santa Maria Maggiore altarpiece*, in *Studien zur Toskanischen Kunst: Festschrift für Ludwig Heinrich Heydenreich*, München 1964, pp. 169-190; J. Shearman, *Masaccio's Pisa Altarpiece: an Alternative Reconstruction*, in «The Burlington Magazine», CVIII (1966), pp. 449-455; J. Polzer, *The anatomy of Masaccio's Holy Trinity*, in «Jahrbuch der Berliner Museen», 93 (1971); C. Gardner von Teuffel, *Masaccio and the Pisa Altarpiece: A New Approach*, in «Jahrbuch der Berliner Museen», 1977, pp. 23-68; U. Baldini, *Nuovi affreschi nella Cappella Brancacci. Masaccio e Masolino*, in «Critica d'arte», n.s., 1 (1984), pp. 65-72; U. Baldini, *Restauro alla Cappella Brancacci, primi risultati*, in «Critica d'arte», n.s., 9 (1986), pp. 65-68; C. Brandon Strehlke and M. Tucker, *The Santa Maria Maggiore altarpiece: New observations*, in «Arte cristiana», LXXV (1987), pp. 105-24; P. Joannides, *The Colonna Triptych by Masolino and Masaccio: Collaboration and chronology*, in «Arte cristiana», LXXVI (1988), pp. 339-346.

Monographs: A. von Schmarsow, *Masaccio Studien*, Kassel 1895-1899; B. Berenson, *Florentine Painters of the Renaissance*, New York-London 1896; E. Somarè, *Masaccio*, Milano 1924; H. Lindberg, *To the problem of Masolino and Masaccio*, Stockholm 1931; M. Salmi, *Masaccio*, Roma 1932 and Milano 1948; U. Procacci, *Tutta la pittura di Masaccio*, Milano 1951; L. Berti, *Masaccio*, Milano 1964; L. Berti, P. Volponi, *L'opera completa di Masaccio*, Milano 1968; J. Beck with G. Corti, *Masaccio: the Documents*, Locust Valley 1978; U. Baldini, O. Casazza, *La Cappella Brancacci*, Milano 1990; P. Joannides, *Masaccio and Masolino. A complete Catalogue*, London 1993; J.T. Spike, *Masaccio*, Milano 1995 (2002[2]); R. Goffen, *Masaccio's Trinity*, Cambridge 1998; *Masaccio 1422. Il Trittico di San Giovenale e il suo tempo*, edited by C. Caneva, Milano 2001; *The Panel Paintings of Masolino and Masaccio. The Role of Technique*, edited by C. Brandon Strehlke and C. Frosinini, Milano 2002; *The Cambridge Companion to Masaccio*, edited by D. Cole Ahl, Cambridge University Press 2002; *La Trinità di Masaccio. Il restauro dell'anno Duemila*, edited by C. Danti, Firenze 2002; *Masaccio e Masolino. Il gioco delle parti*, Milano 2002.
Catalogues: *L'età di Masaccio. Il primo Quattrocento a Firenze*, edited by L. Berti and A. Paolucci, Firenze 1990; *Nel segno di Masaccio: l'invenzione della prospettiva*, edited by F. Camerota, Firenze 2001; *Masaccio e i pittori del suo tempo agli Uffizi*, edited by A. Cecchi with the collaboration of L. Aquino, Milano 2002; *Masaccio e le origini del Rinascimento*, edited by L. Bellosi with the collaboration of L. Cavazzini and A. Galli, Milano 2002.

PHOTOGRAPHIC ACKNOWLEDGEMENTS

All the photographs are from the Giunti Archive except:
12a, 24, 25, 31 (Giunti Archive/Photo Rabatti & Domingie); 46 (courtesy Opificio delle Pietre Dure, Florence); 15, 44-45, 47 (Antonio Quattrone, Florence); cover, 17, 35 (Rabatti & Domingie Photography, Florence).

As concerns rights to reproduction, the publisher is willing to pay any amounts due for photographs for which it has been impossible to determine the source.